COACHES GUIDE TO
SPORT
LAW

ACEP Level 2 Sport Science Courses

ACEP Level 2 sport science courses are available to accompany the following texts:

Coaches Guide to Sport Law by Gary Nygaard and Thomas H. Boone. The authors explain a coach's legal responsibilities in easy to understand terms and give practical advice for improving standards of care and safety for athletes.

Coaches Guide to Time Management by Charles Kozoll. This innovative text shows coaches how to improve their self-organization and how to avoid the harmful effects of stress by controlling the pressures inherent in many coaching programs.

Coaches Guide to Sport Physiology by Brian Sharkey leads coaches step-by-step through the development of fitness-training programs suitable for their sport and for the athletes they coach.

Coaches Guide to Sport Injuries by David Bergeron and Holly Wilson gives coaches information on injury prevention and on the immediate treatment and follow-up care for common athletic injuries.

Coaches Guide to Teaching Sport Skills by Bob Christina and Steven Houseworth uses practical coaching examples to take coaches through the teaching/learning process and offers coaches valuable advice for improving their teaching effectiveness.

Coaches Guide to Sport Psychology by Rainer Martens presents information on motivation, communication, stress management, the use of mental imagery, and other fascinating topics for enhancing coach-athlete relationships and for stimulating improved sport performances.

Each course consists of a *Coaches Guide*, a *Study Guide*, and a *Workbook*. ACEP certification is awarded for successful course completion. For more information about these courses, write to:

ACEP Level 2
Box 5076
Champaign, IL 61820
(217)351-5076

COACHES GUIDE TO SPORT LAW

A publication for the
American Coaching Effectiveness Program
Level 2 Sport Science Curriculum

Gary Nygaard, PhD
University of Montana

Thomas H. Boone, JD
Boone, Karlberg & Haddon
Missoula, Montana

HUMAN KINETICS PUBLISHERS, INC.
Champaign, Illinois

Library of Congress Cataloging in Publication Data

Nygaard, Gary, 1941-
    Coaches guide to sport law.

    Bibliography: p.
    Includes index.
        1. Liability for sports accidents—United States.
2. Coaches (Athletics)—Legal status, laws, etc.—
United States.   I. Boone, Thomas H.   II. Title.
KF1290.S66N93   1985   346.7303′22   84-25284
ISBN 0-931250-94-3   347.306322

Developmental Editor: Stephen C. Jefferies
Copy Editor: Olga Murphy
Typesetters: Sandra Meier and Aurora Garcia
Text Layout: Janet K. Davenport
Illustrator: Jerry Barrett
Cover Design and Layout: Jack W. Davis

ISBN: 0-931250-94-3
Copyright © 1985 by Gary Nygaard and Thomas H. Boone

Printed in the United States of America

10 9 8 7 6 5 4 3 2 1

Human Kinetics Publishers, Inc.
Box 5076, Champaign, IL 61820

Contents

Preface

This legal guide was written for sport instructors, especially coaches and physical educators. More lawsuits than ever before are directed at coaches' actions and inactions on playing fields and in gymnasiums. Lawyers, judges, and juries are carefully scrutinizing coaches' behaviors to determine the presence or absence of negligence.

This guide focuses on the legal responsibilities of coaches and physical educators, but much of the content is equally applicable to those who teach sports skills in other recreational settings. Through an increasing number of lawsuits, the courts are providing coaches with guidelines for acceptable behavior; therefore, it is vital that you become familiar with these guidelines.

In easy-to-read terms, this guide presents the legal duties you have as a coach. The content is drawn from a thorough review of sport lawsuits (or sports injury litigation) which we have conducted over the past 8 years.

When coaching or teaching movement activities, you must balance fun and learning with safety. Every sport, every form of human movement contains a potential risk of injury. Coaches must do more than ever before to reduce this risk, especially of those injuries not directly related to the sport or activity. *The risks of a game (called inherent risks) are acceptable as long as coaches act prudently and as long as these inherent risks are known, appreciated, understood, and consciously accepted by the participants.* Other risks are not acceptable. If one of your baseball players slides into second base and sprains an ankle, that is part of the game; but if he slides into second base and sprains an ankle because his spikes catch on an old base stake that was not removed, he may have good cause to bring suit. This guide will help you distinguish between the inherent risks, those that are acceptable, in the sports and activities you coach and teach, and those that are not. A Sport Law Course, which uses this book and an accompanying study guide, is available from the American Coaching Effectiveness Program (ACEP).

The more sensitive you are to creating a safe environment, the safer your athletes will be. The more knowledge you have of your legal responsibilities, the smaller the chance of you being sued. The more you digest the information in this book, the better coach you will become.

No game was ever worth a rap
For a rational man to play,
Into which no accident, no mishap
Could possibly find its way.

Adam Lindsay Gordon

Chapter 1
Negligence and a Coach's Legal Duties

INTRODUCTION

Dangers of Using Improper Techniques

You are coaching baseball. One of your players, Bill, who has had considerable coaching prior to making your high school junior varsity team, had been repeatedly taught by you and his previous coaches to slide feet-first into a base. He had never been taught to slide head-first. Two weeks ago, Bill used his shoulder to "bowl over" a catcher and score a run, and you congratulated him. Later, Bill was on third base and you flashed him the sign for a "squeeze play." The batter missed his bunt attempt, and in trying to knock the ball out of the catcher's grip, Bill ran into the catcher head-first and suffered a serious injury.

You are sued on the basis that you failed to provide adequate and competent coaching and that you carelessly and negligently trained, supervised, managed, and controlled the injured player because he slid head-first. Remember, the sliding technique you taught Bill was exclusively the feet-first slide. Were you negligent in any way in this case?

1

This actual case from New York was reported at a conference on sport injury lawsuits. The results were conflicting. The Supreme Court of Queens County found that even though the coach taught the proper technique consistently and correctly, he failed to warn the player of the dangers involved in sliding head-first. He failed to adequately warn his players of the dangers of using an improper technique. The Court awarded the young man $1,800,000. On appeal, the Supreme Court, Appellate Division, agreed with the findings of fact in the case but reduced the award to $1,000,000. On further appeal 3 years after the injury, the Court of Appeals reversed and dismissed the case, finding no negligence (*Passantino v. Board of Education of City of New York*, 1976). These judgments illustrate one of the perplexing truths about lawsuits resulting from sports injuries: The law is whatever it decides to be on a given day.

Recently, a Seattle, Washington, school was sued because a player became a quadriplegic when he lowered his head using his helmet to make contact. Because he had never instructed his players to make contact with the helmet, the coach's failure was not in teaching the improper technique. The coach's failure was his lack of sufficient warning of the danger of using the helmet in making contact. The jury's award in this case was $6,300,000.

These two examples illustrate just one of the duties you have. *Not only must you provide a safe playing area, proper equipment, competent supervision, and adequate instruction, you must also warn your players of the danger of using improper techniques.* You will learn more about this in chapter 4; however, we mention it now because it exemplifies how our judicial system is prescribing what is acceptable and unacceptable coaching behavior.

Frequency of Warnings

Consider another example. Jeff, a high school trampolinist, reports to workout with a cold and a stuffy nose. You, his coach, had earlier warned all members of the team to tell you if they were ill or injured. Jeff does not think his relatively minor illness worth mentioning, and while executing a body twist in mid-air, he loses his equilibrium and falls, receiving a serious cervical (neck) injury. Did you comply with your duty to adequately warn Jeff?

Trial magazine (Langerman & Fidel, 1977), which used this example, did not believe so. For a warning to be heeded, you should have given the warning frequently with a clear explanation of the harm which might result from failure to comply. You should have taken elaborate care to assure that your athletes understood the effect a modest cold or stuffy nose could have on the intricate balance gymnasts need to twist through the air. According to *Trial*, you violated one of the specific duties of a coach. You could be negligent.

NEGLIGENCE

There are many different kinds of lawsuits in sport and physical education. Some have been criminal lawsuits, and some civil rights lawsuits (especially in recent years), but most of your concern as a coach is with lawsuits alleging negligence on your part. What does the term "negligence" mean to you as a coach? Basically, *negligence is when a coach fails to act as a reasonable and a prudent coach would act in a similar situation.* Should you be sued and brought to trial, a judge or jury determines the appropriateness of your behavior. Most judges and most members of juries are not likely to be trained coaches. This creates the definite possibility that people with a limited understanding of the pressures, demands, and concerns you have as a coach will evaluate your professional behavior.

Four factors are considered in assessing whether or not a coach is negligent. All four of these factors must be present for negligence to be determined.

The Presence of a Duty

Do you owe your players a duty? Yes, you owe them a number of duties; these duties are explained later in this chapter. Most of the rest of this guide will explain these duties and offer suggestions to help you execute each of your duties more effectively.

Breaching that Duty

Was that duty breached? Did you fail to do something you should have done? Did you do the wrong thing? Did you do the proper thing, but do it incorrectly? If the answer to any one of these three questions is yes, the likelihood of being considered negligent increases.

What Caused the Injury?

Was your breach of duty responsible for the player's injuries? The court will examine the relationship between the breach of your duty and the resulting injury and will try to determine if your breach of duty was a substantial factor in the injury to the player. Intervening factors, such as the behavior of a third party and some negligence on the part of the injured player, may exist. These factors will both be weighed and evaluated in respect to your breach of duty.

Extent of Injuries

What is the extent of actual injury or damage? If a quadriplegic is wheeled into the courtroom, you can imagine the dramatic effect on a judge and jury. If the damage is emotional strain or harassment, the damage will not be as apparent but can still be determined to be present.

Remember, all *four* of these factors must be proven before you can be found negligent. If any one of these factors is absent, liability will not be found.

LEGAL DEFENSES

Should you be charged with negligence, two common defenses are likely to be used. These defenses may limit liability even if you are found to have been negligent. The first of these defenses is called *assumption of risk*, and the second is called *contributory negligence*.

Assumption of Risks

Every sport has inherent risks, and it is certainly possible for players to subject themselves to those risks. However, your players must *know, understand, and appreciate* those risks. You must clearly inform and repeatedly remind your players of these risks and minimize them as much as possible. In racquetball, for example, being struck by the ball is a risk. The ball can travel at speeds in excess of 120 miles per hour and can pose a serious threat to players if they are struck in the eye. Not only must you explain this to your racquetball players, you must also remind them repeatedly not to look at the ball when it is being struck and to always wear acceptable eyeguards. When you teach racquetball, make sure all players have their eyeguards on before playing. If they do not, remind them of the danger, emphasize that no game is worth an eye, and insist they immediately put on their eyeguards, keeping them on for the duration of the game. If a player does not comply with your instructions, it would be unwise to allow him or her to continue playing.

Contributory Negligence

The second common defense, contributory negligence, means the player acted negligently and contributed to the injury. In our racquetball example, if after you insisted Jenny put on her eyeguards, and she removed them as soon as you moved to another court, then she herself contributed to any eye injury that occurred.

In many states the presence of contributory negligence bars recovery even though the coach may have been negligent as well. Furthermore, the negligence of each party is not compared in order to determine which party is more at fault.

Comparative Negligence Laws

Recently, however, some states have modified these harsh interpretations and have adopted *comparative negligence laws*. In these states the negligence of the parties is compared on a percentage basis. Although there are exceptions, generally, under a comparative negligence statute, a player cannot recover if his or her negligence contributes 50% or more to the accident.

Other Defenses

Other defenses are used occasionally, such as an Act of God and a variety of technical defenses, but your most likely defense is either assumption of risk or contributory negligence. In any case, you want to avoid having to use any defense: You do not want to be charged with negligence.

Let's now learn what duties you owe your players. Then we will turn our attention to each of those duties and see what you must do to be more reasonable and prudent in your behavior as a coach.

Clearly, the courts are more demanding of coaches today, and the public expects coaches to behave according to these standards. Consequently, there are more sport-related lawsuits than ever before. We may bemoan this increase in litigation, especially when it appears to be frivolous, but some coaches deserve to be sued. In one instance, a coach used chemically active lime to line a football field which resulted in a player's loss of vision. In another instance, a coach permitted an initiation ceremony which required each player to lie on electric wires with a jar of water on his chest; one player was electrocuted. You would hopefully not make such blatant errors, but would you have known to warn Bill about sliding head-first into home? *It is essential that you know what the judicial system expects of you as a coach!*

LEGAL DUTIES OF COACHES

Remember, one of the factors necessary for negligence is the presence of a legal duty, and coaches have legal duties to their athletes. As you coach, you have certain legal duties you must perform reasonably and prudently. The judicial system expects you to provide seven major duties to the young people who play under your direction. In addition, you must consider other factors which, while not duties, can influence how you perform your legal duties. Each of these duties is described next and then discussed more extensively in later chapters.

Adequate Supervision

First, you must provide *adequate supervision*. Supervision is of two types: general and specific. Of the two, your specific supervision of the action in games or practices is usually the more important.

Sound Planning

A second duty you owe your players is *good, sound planning*. Progression is essential. You must plan your skill instruction, your practices, and your drills so that your players do not move too rapidly into techniques, scrimmages, or contests which are beyond their skill levels. Obviously, you want your players to improve, but this improvement should not be coerced nor forced on a player.

Inherent Risks

Third, you must warn players of the *inherent risks in the sport* and of the dangers of using questionable techniques. Repeat these warnings sufficiently so that your players know, understand, and appreciate the risks they may encounter.

Safe Playing Environment

Your fourth duty, and a very important one, is to provide *a safe environment* for practice and play. This does not just include the playing field and gymnasium, but also includes the proper use of equipment. It is your responsibility to inspect your facility and equipment regularly and thoroughly.

Evaluating Athletes' Disabilities

You must evaluate your players for injuries or incapacities and determine any limitations on participation caused by that injury or incapacity. You have some demanding tasks related to this fifth duty, which include trying to ascertain the mental condition of your players and perhaps even noting possible cases of child abuse.

Matching or Equating Opponents

A sixth coaching duty is *to fairly match or equate players for practice or competitive conditions*. Failing to properly match participants has resulted in negligence in such a safe and easy lead-up game as line soccer. The more body contact your sport generates, the more careful you must be in matching participants.

Emergency First Aid Procedures

The seventh duty you have is *to provide proper first aid and to establish emergency medical procedures that can be put immediately into action*. We will discuss two classic cases in which football coaches failed to carry out this duty and were found to be negligent.

Specific Legal Concerns

In addition to these duties, our judicial system requires you to make other decisions. You must *assure that the basic civil rights of your participants are not violated*. It is no longer as easy for you to place restrictions on the appearance or expression of your players. In the event of a dispute, follow the basic principles of due process; your players' rights follow them onto the playing field. You also must consider other factors related to the game you coach, specifically the *spectators as well as the game officials* you use. Furthermore, keep *good records*, particularly in the event of an injury.

General Legal Concerns

Also, be knowledgeable of some guidelines concerning *transportation and insurance*. You definitely need to be aware of the risks of various forms of transporting players, especially when using personal vehicles.

Sport lawsuits can involve large amounts of money and can put a person in financial ruin. Therefore, it is a wise idea for *all coaches to carry adequate personal liability insurance*. You can purchase large amounts of personal liability insurance at reasonable rates from a variety of sources. We will tell you about these sources and the limitations of which to be aware in these liability policies in chapter 10.

RECOMMEN-DATIONS

This chapter outlined how to be a reasonable and a prudent coach. In the following chapters, each of the legal duties of a coach is thoroughly discussed. Each chapter will begin by considering the importance of this duty from your standpoint and will cite examples of specific court cases. Whenever possible, we will give specific recommendations to aid you in performing your duties. In some instances, however, specific recommendations are not possible; instead, we will inform you of the general recommendations our judicial system is making.

The law is not static: It is dynamic. It varies depending on locale, on applicable state law, on the makeup of a jury, on the persuasiveness of attorneys, on different local precedents, on changes in attitudes, on changes in a sport, and on other numerous factors. Remember, what was negligent in one situation might not be perceived so in another, and what was reasonable and prudent behavior in 1966 might not be today. For all of these reasons, our recommendations are just that—recommendations. They are not and cannot be completely definitive. The state of sport injury litigation prohibits absolute precision.

Chapter 2
Supervision

WHAT IS SUPERVISION?

Supervision simply means you are in charge of others as they carry out some act. As a coach, it means you are in charge of your assistant coaches and your players before, during, and after practices and games. Supervision also means you have responsibilities to your players. Actually, supervision entails all of the legal duties discussed in this guide: planning, presenting warnings, providing a safe place to play, evaluating for injury or incapacity, matching for equitable competition, and providing first aid and procedures for emergency medical care. In addition, and most importantly, supervision means you must closely supervise the activity you are teaching or coaching. Indeed, of all your legal duties to your players, specific supervision is your most important.

Your responsibility to supervise involves two different but related forms of supervision. You have *general supervisory duties* and *specific supervisory duties*. The difference between the two is simple: General supervision is the supervision of all the areas and activities related to the game or activity, and specific supervision is the supervision of the game, practice, or activity itself.

GENERAL SUPERVISION

In your general supervisory duties you are responsible for more than just what happens on the practice or game field. You also are responsible for locker rooms, shower rooms, equipment rooms, and other adjacent areas. This poses a sticky problem for those of you who coach coeducational activities or who coach a team composed of members of the opposite sex. When and under what conditions may you enter the locker room of participants of the opposite sex? How do you supervise this locker room?

Here is an example of the problem. We received a call one day from a parent of a young boy who was participating in a coeducational physical education class. The teacher of the class was a female, so a senior male student was assigned to supervise the boys' locker room. The mother claimed her son was frequently beaten by this male student supervisor. That certainly was not proper general supervision, and the problem was quickly resolved.

School Sport Programs

General supervision is especially a problem at the beginning and the end of practices when players are arriving or leaving; some are showering, some dressing, some checking out equipment, some being taped, and others waiting in the practice area. You have general supervisory responsibilities for all these areas. Because of the nature of school sports, general supervision is more of a concern for those who coach in these institutions than for those who coach in nonschool sport programs. The following cases are but three of the numerous examples of failure to carry out this duty of general supervision.

Inadequate Supervision

CASE 1: A physical education department in California was assigned the responsibility for supervising a parking lot area adjacent to the gymnasium during the noon lunch period (*Dailey v. Los Angeles Unified School District*, 1970). While the members of the physical education staff were aware of this responsibility, no formal plan of general supervision was developed. One day, the teacher who was to supervise the area was eating his lunch at a desk. He had his back to the window looking out over the parking lot, and a wall partially obstructed his view of this area where several students had gathered, and where two had engaged in "slap-boxing." As one of the participants was hit, he fell backwards, struck his head on the asphalt, and later died as a result of this injury. The school was held responsible for the negligent acts of their agents, the physical education staff, because of its failure to develop and implement an adequate plan for general supervision.

CASE 2: A teacher in Oregon had two students remove a springboard from the play area into the equipment area

(*Grant v. Lake Oswego School District*, 1974). They moved it partway into the area but failed to place it on its side. Upon reentering the play area, one of the students jumped off of the springboard and struck her head on the door jam. Negligence was found due to inadequate general supervision.

CASE 3: A young boy in New Jersey injured his hands sliding down a rope (*Miller v. Cloidt and Board of Education of the Borough of Chatham*, 1964). The physical education teacher took the boy to the first aid room after warning the other participants not to perform on any apparatus until he returned. One student did and, as a result, suffered a crippling injury. Negligence was found, because had the teacher remained in the participation area, the injury would not have occurred. In carrying out one duty, he failed to carry out the other (specific supervision). The initial award in this early 1960s case was in excess of $1,000,000.

How to Supervise Properly

General supervision is necessary in playground situations as well as the other areas mentioned in the preceding paragraphs. In performing your general supervision duty, you must be close enough to the area to see and to hear what is occurring. Also, have a written plan for general supervision. If you have assistant coaches or aides, or even responsible players, they can assist you in carrying out this duty if you train them to do so. Write out the procedure for how they will assist you in this duty and have your supervisor approve it. Then when training others for general supervisory duties, have them take into consideration (a) what to look for; (b) what to listen for; (c) where to stand; (d) how to move around; and (e) what to do if a problem arises. You must consider all of

these factors when you have others share your responsibility for general supervision.

SPECIFIC SUPERVISION

Specific supervision is the close supervision of an activity when your athletes are performing that activity. Specific supervision is required when you are instructing an activity for the first time and when the activity is especially dangerous. As a general rule, the more dangerous the activity, the closer your supervision must be. Gymnastics requires more stringent specific supervision than golf, simply because of the nature of the two sports.

Specific supervision also becomes necessary when conditions make a safe activity more dangerous. For example, if you are coaching golf and inclement weather forces you indoors, then closer supervision is required. A Nebraska lawsuit illustrates this situation. Golf is not that dangerous of a sport, but because of the manner in which the sport was taught indoors, a young man was struck by a golf club and killed. Because one of the specific supervisory errors made was a change from an approved and written plan for teaching indoor golf, this case will be described in more detail in chapter 3 on planning.

Dangers of Unsupervised Activity

What does specific supervision require of you? What are some considerations you must make for specifically supervising your sport? First, *we strongly recommend that you do not leave a practice or game unattended.* Although your absence, of and by itself, may not be negligence, if an injury occurs and you are not present, your absence will be examined to determine if it was a substantial factor contributing to the injury that occurred. This is important enough to reiterate: *Do not* leave a practice or game unattended.

In a Wisconsin case, the instructor, for no apparent reason, left a class of over 40 boys unattended (*Cirillo v. Board of Education*, 1967). It became a roughhouse game, and an injury occurred. The court held that the teacher's presence would have prevented the game from becoming too rough. In a 1953 California case, however, a tennis coach had a late afternoon physical education class consisting primarily of players on his tennis team (*Wright v. San Bernardino High School District*, 1953). Because he had to prepare the draw for an upcoming tournament, he left to do so after instructing his students to play a modified form of handball. Some did, but others started to play a modified form of baseball with their tennis racquets and tennis balls. A young man was struck in the eye and suffered a moderately severe eye injury. The court held that, in this case, the teacher/coach had a valid reason for his absence and that the same injury could have occurred had he been present. Consequently, he was not negligent. We feel this was an unusual decision, and had the same case been tried today, a different conclusion might well have been reached.

Qualified Supervisors

You must also consider who can be a valid supervisor. Many sports are coached by individuals with limited training, especially in nonschool sports. Because of budgetary restrictions, other sport programs use untrained personnel as head or assistant coaches. Parents frequently help in coaching young children's teams. In schools, students and student teachers are frequently given supervisory responsibility in physical education classes and athletic programs. Is it acceptable for you to assign supervisory responsibilities to parents, untrained assistants, or older players?

Everyone who coaches must not necessarily be a certified coach, but it is necessary that everyone who coaches knows what is expected of him or her. The concept of shared responsibility is important here. Any responsible person can help you to coach a sport, but all assistants must be competent and understand the legal duties that affect them as your assistants.

To be competent, supervisors must know how to

1. supervise the activity,
2. plan,
3. present clear warnings of the risks of an activity,
4. help in providing a safe environment,
5. be able to evaluate injury or incapacity,

6. properly match participants, and

7. administer first aid and put the emergency medical system into operation.

Essentially, you are responsible for training those untrained individuals helping you coach your sport. Your assistants and you, of course, must have a clear understanding of the scope of their duties and responsibilities to your athletes.

Using Supervisors

A second consideration in performing your specific supervisory duties is to determine how many supervisors are needed, how many you have, and where they should be located. Assume you have one assistant coach for your team. This may or may not be enough depending on the sport. If it is not enough, you should try to acquire more. Then your responsibility is to make certain they are competent and aware of their legal duties to your players.

As an example, assume you are coaching basketball and have 20 players trying out for your team. You need and are able to find and train one more assistant coach. How will you use your assistant coaches? Where will they be during the tryouts, and what will they be doing? How can you best use yourself and your assistants to provide the best care and coaching for your players?

One of the reasons for negligence in the golf class in which the young man was killed was the improper location of a student teacher. Instead of being in a position where he could see all of the indoor practice mats, he was focusing his attention on one mat and on one group of players. This case violated the accepted plan of the school district for teaching golf indoors. In the court's opinion, the student teacher was in the wrong place. The essential consideration you have to make is how to best use yourself and your assistants so that the sport can be well coached, safely.

Identifying Dangerous Activities

When specifically supervising an activity, you also must consider the nature of the activity, the way it breaks down into different skills and techniques, and the way this affects supervision. Some types of play, some drills, and some activities are more dangerous than others and require more immediate attention from you and your assistants.

For example, you are coaching racquetball, and you introduce some of your players to doubles play. Because you have four players and four racquets instead of two in a 20' x 20' x 40' space, doubles is obviously more dangerous than singles. In addition, if this is the players' first experience with doubles, specific supervision is required. Thus, you should closely watch and possibly officiate the first few games of doubles, focusing your attention on the new, more dangerous activity.

Another example: You are coaching a football team with your two assistants, and your players are engaged in blocking drills, tackling drills, passing drills, kicking drills, and wind sprints in five different groups. Which of these groups are going to require your closest attention? In which of these groups is an injury most likely to occur? It might be safer to break the activity down differently. How could you rearrange it so that you and your two assistants could better supervise the riskier activities of your sport?

Closeness to the Activity

In performing your duties of specific supervision, you must consider three additional points. The first is to determine how close to the activity you need to be. The boxing coach who sat in the bleachers and watched two relatively inexperienced boxers go at it was too far away. The football coach who was run over by his players as they ran an off-tackle play was probably too close. You need to consider a variety of factors in determining your distance: These include the danger of the activity, the size, age, and maturity of your players, and whether they are beginners, intermediate, or advanced performers. Stay close enough to supervise, but do not get in the way.

Recognizing Warning Signs

Second, try to develop a feel for warning signs during an activity. You need to be able to determine (a) when aggressive play becomes too aggressive; (b) when your players' "creativity" in technique becomes dirty play or dangerous; and (c) when teasing and horseplay become malicious. You also need to develop a sense of impending trouble, for example, of knowing when your basketball player is too forceful when he is blocking with his elbows. When you sense this, it is imperative that you stop play, let things cool down, review the technique at hand, and then watch very closely as play resumes. In essence, you need to develop the ability to recognize and stop the danger signs of an activity. To do this, you must know your activity and your players well and use what we call "preventive supervision."

Establishing Stop Signals

Finally, very early in your program, you should establish a "stop signal." This is a signal you use when you must immediately suspend play or practice. Some sports already have these stop signals built into them.

In golf, for example, the word "fore" is a stop signal. One of the first things we teach in golf is the proper use of the word: "If you hear it, duck; if you hit the ball toward someone, yell it out." A problem that we have encountered with this stop signal is that so many beginning golfers are embarrassed to use it; if they hit a ball toward someone, they murmur "fore" and then look the other way or attempt to hide behind their golf bag. That word must be used forcefully and immediately. We have yet to teach a golf class where we have not had to stop practice and remind everyone to duck if they hear it and yell if they have hit at someone.

Most sports do not have such stop signals built into their structure, so you need to find one. It should be a special signal, one that will immediately catch the attention of your players, and one that has only one interpretation: "Stop!" You probably use or have access to a whistle in your program. Make sure it works loudly, and then inform your players that if they hear your signal (e.g., three loud, short blasts of the whistle), they are immediately to stop whatever they are doing and turn their attention to you. Remember, acoustics are poor in many gymnasiums, pools, and playing fields, so develop a stop signal that is effective.

RECOMMEN-DATIONS

We have made a number of recommendations in this chapter regarding general and specific supervision. Remember, supervision is your most important duty and encompasses all the other duties yet to be discussed, so review the following recommendations carefully:

1. When the situation requires only general supervision, be sure you or your assistants have planned for it and are located so you can see and hear all the activities in the area.

2. Specific supervision, the close supervision of an activity, is required whenever the activity poses risk to your players. It also is required if the activity is new and when conditions make a safe activity more dangerous. The more dangerous the activity, the closer it must be observed and supervised.

3. Do not leave a practice or game unattended. Make sure someone competent is present.

4. Because the final responsibility for safe coaching is yours, be absolutely sure your assistants are competent in the sport and are aware of the legal duties associated with coaching that sport.

5. Check that you have an adequate number of supervisors for the activities practiced or played, and be sure your supervisors are located in the best location to supervise.

6. Thoroughly understand how your sport breaks down into different skills and techniques and the effect this has on supervision. Some parts of an activity are more

dangerous than others, so you must watch them more closely.

7. Don't be too close to the activity nor too far away. You can supervise some sports by watching; others require "hands-on" supervision.

8. Develop a feel for the warning signs of an activity which may lead to an injury so that you can take precautionary action.

9. Have a loud, clear stop signal that is understood by all of your players so that when they hear it, they stop play immediately.

Supervision is a broad term, and it entails many different responsibilities. It means you must closely watch the activity at hand, and it also means you must fulfill the legal duties described here and those discussed in the rest of this guide.

Chapter 3
Planning

PLANNING AHEAD

Planning should precede everything when you coach a sport. It is no longer proper for you to "throw out the ball" and let things happen. Your plans must be reasonable, well thought out, and based on the past experiences and readiness of your athletes. Your plans should be updated continuously. Most importantly, because you may be asked to prove you have planned, your plans should be written and retained. Writing the plan effectively is important; this chapter will give you some good advice, and the *Sport Law Study Guide* (Jefferies, 1985) will show you how to apply this advice in your own program.

A word of caution first: Do not think of each of these legal duties as being separate and distinct from each other. As we mentioned in chapter 2, all of your duties are supervisory duties. It is also true that all of your duties require planning. Coaches need a plan for supervision, a plan to present warnings, a plan to provide a safe environment, a plan to evaluate their players for injury or incapacity, a plan to match or equate their players, a plan to administer first aid and start the emergency medical system, and, yes, a plan to plan. All of these duties overlap and affect one another, and all are the coach's legal duties. Remember, negligence may be the result of poor planning or of the way you carry out the plan. Poor planning, of course, increases the likelihood of poor execution. But even perfectly designed plans are of no value unless you carry them out in a reasonable and a prudent fashion.

CASE EXAMPLES

Improper Planning

A New York case involved the simple game of line soccer (*Keesee v. Board of Education of the City of New York*, 1962).

An approved syllabus was used for the class, but in teaching the activity, the physical education teacher deviated from this approved plan in at least seven ways. The participants had played this game once before on the 60' x 50' gymnasium floor. The instructor divided the class into two teams of 20 to 22 girls each, and then numbered them 1 through 4 so that when one number was called, four students from each team would race out toward the center line and attempt to gain possession of the ball. The syllabus, however, had recommended that players be given consecutive numbers so that only two players would be kicking at the ball, and that play commence at the center of the court so that two players would stand and face each other at center court.

During the course of play, a young girl was injured. Because the game had deviated so much from the syllabus (which also had stated that the game was only for boys), negligence was found. In this case, the plan was adequate and even though it was not the best plan, it had been approved by a supervisor. The "spur of the moment" changes resulted in a determination that the instructor had been negligent. Remember, if you do change established and approved plans, get your new plan approved.

Improper Execution of an Approved Plan

A similar example occurred in Nebraska in 1979 (*Brahatcek v. Millard School District No. 17*, 1979). A 14-year-old freshman in high school was struck and killed by a golf club swung by a fellow student. In this case, mandatory golf instruction during physical education began on a Monday. The decedent was absent from school that day, so his first exposure to the golf activity with his class was on the following Wednesday, the day of the accident. Classes on both dates were held inside because of inclement weather. The class was coeducational with one male teacher, one female teacher, and a male student teacher. The school had an approved plan for indoor golf instruction which the instructors revised to enable more students to take part, but they failed to get the change approved. (We feel that their revision of the plan was actually better than the approved plan.)

On Wednesday, the male teacher was absent, so the female instructor and the male student teacher taught the class. While the female instructor remained in a position where she could see all of the mats, the student teacher focused his attention on one mat in the center of the line of mats used for instruction. Thus positioned, he could not see what was occurring at one of the end mats where the decedent was having difficulty. Because the decedent had never held a golf club in his hand, he asked a fellow student to help him. Looking over his shoulder, the student helper saw that the decedent had moved about 10 feet away. He took two practice swings, then stepped up to the whiffle ball, and took a full swing at it. Unaware that the decedent had moved closer, he hit his friend in the head on the follow-through. Two days later, he died.

The student teacher acknowledged it was not until after the accident that he realized the class arrangement was different from what was recommended: he had received no instruction from any of the regular teachers prior to the golf class; he did not have a lesson plan; and he did not give any oral instructions to any of the students as a whole. An expert witness for the decedent testified that he would have used a more conservative plan for indoor golf instruction, such as the previous plan which had been approved. He testified that the teachers should have been watching all the mats and that if the teacher noticed a student having difficulty or needing specialized instruction, the teacher should have called the class to a halt and demonstrated to the one student in need while all the other students watched and listened. Negligence was found and an award of $50,000 was made to the estate of the deceased student.

Poor Planning

A letterman's club initiation ceremony in South Dakota illustrates poor planning (*Degooyer v. Harkness*, 1944). At this annual initiation, each candidate for membership was given an electric shock, produced by means of running electric wires connected with batteries through a current reducing transformer. In the 1941 initiation ceremony, however, the transformer was not available, and the electric current was obtained not from batteries, but from an electric light socket. Each boy was brought separately into the room, asked to lie on an electrically wired mat, and then had a glass of water placed upon his chest. When the current was turned on, the boy receiving the shock would respond, the glass of water either spilling over him or onto the floor. In this ceremony, the fourth candidate complained that the electric shock was very strong. Regardless, the next candidate was brought into the room, placed upon the wired mat, and given this electric shock. The initiate died immediately. The court found the coach supervising the ceremony negligent.

Lack of Planning

A recent Illinois case illustrates a lack of planning (*Landers v. School District No. 203*, 1978). In this instance, a 15-year-old girl received serious injuries to her neck while attempting to perform a backward somersault. On the day prior to the injury, the girl told the instructor after the physical education class that she was afraid to do the backward somersault because she did not know how to perform it. The teacher offered to help her after school, but because the student was riding the school bus, this was not possible.

The next day, the teacher told her to practice the exercise. The girl said that she could not, reminding the instructor of her offer to help her. The instructor replied she could not help immediately, and suggested the student get another student to assist her. She did, tried the backward somersault, and received her injury. She brought suit, and negligence was found. The court ruled that in her lack of planning for the instruction of this particular student, the teacher showed an utter indifference to the safety of the student.

These are but a few of the examples of improper planning in sport and physical education lawsuits. Most sport injury litigation involves improper planning to meet a coach's legal duties. Even though the focus might be on another more specific duty, the question of improper planning may still be raised. Good planning should be evident in all that you do as a coach. Next, we consider those factors that are essential to proper planning.

CONSIDERATIONS IN PLANNING

Written Plans

It is a good idea to have your plans in written form. If possible, develop your plans with your colleagues and then have your athletic director or immediate supervisor approve them. Be very careful if you deviate from these plans once they have been written. As the previous examples illustrate, courts tend to look askance at spur-of-the-moment changes in plans, particularly if there is no need for a change. *Develop a sound, justifiable plan and carry it through. Evaluate your plans periodically and adapt them as warranted.*

Performance Objectives

Your plans should be written in terms of the participant's performance. These performance objectives should indicate that you are more concerned with what the participants will be doing rather than with what you will be teaching. Instead of stating, "I will teach you the backward somersault," write, "By the end of this practice, each of you will be able to perform the backward somersault." By doing this, your participants will have a clearer understanding of what is expected of them and will, perhaps, be better able to know, understand, and appreciate the risks of the activity. If nothing else, they will probably pay closer attention and ask more questions if they know they will have to perform this activity on this day. Participants should never be forced or coerced into performing an activity if they have valid reservations. But if they know what is expected of them, they will be more likely to express reservations and to ask any questions. If you can prove that your participants knew, understood, and appreciated what they would be doing, you will be better able to defend yourself against a negligence charge.

Reversing the Planning Order

Another good idea is to reverse the apparently logical order of planning by starting at the end and working back toward the beginning. This applies to both long-term and short-term plans and is especially important when you are teaching an activity for the first time. If you start at the beginning and merrily work toward the goal you have in mind, you might discover you have forgotten something or did not allow for sufficient time. Wouldn't it be embarrassing to have your basketball team charge onto the floor for the first game and find itself facing a full court trapping zone defense, a defense you had forgotten about or hadn't had time to cover? As another example, one of our local college football teams used this strategy successfully a few years ago when it instituted the old single-wing offense for a game with its arch-rivals. The plan was totally unexpected, caught the other coaching staff off-guard, and it worked! Because the winning team did have a large, strong quarterback turned running back skillful enough to be a good old-fashioned triple-threat single-wing tailback, perhaps better planning by the losing team would have helped.

Considering the Risks

Your planning process must include a thorough consideration for explaining the risks of the activity. This has become more important in recent years because courts are now asking you to be sure your players know the dangers they face in a sport. All your players must be able to clearly and fully perceive the nature and character of these risks, as well as be fully and sensitively aware of these risks. *They must know, understand, and appreciate the risks of your sport before they can assume those risks, and they must be aware of the risks of the sport before they participate in that sport.*

Using a Waiver

You may think that having the player sign a waiver acknowledging the risks in the sport and relinquishing you of any liability is a good way to protect yourself and your assistants. Although this is not necessarily a bad idea, the next chapter will discuss several severe restrictions on the use of such waivers. Because of the type of players many of you have, such a waiver is of dubious value.

Know Your Sport

This next point may appear trite, but we have observed situations where it has become a factor in poor planning. You must know your subject, your sport, and be current in all its facets. The techniques in sport have changed remarkably in the past two decades (e.g., the Fosbury Flop) and with it the understanding of the effects of sport participation on the human body. *It is your responsibility to be as current as possible in all facets of your sport—both sport-specific knowledge and sports medicine and science knowledge.*

Learning this knowledge once is not good enough; it is also your responsibility to keep abreast of new techniques and new training programs and to determine how appropriate these new techniques and training programs are for your athletes.

If the slider is an effective pitch for major league pitchers, is it appropriate for Little Leaguers, or does it place too much stress on their arms? If college and professional football players run wind sprints during pre-season practices, can your Pop Warner players do the same? Which type of ski boot offers the best protection against knee injuries? You must consider the appropriateness of new ideas in your sport for your athletes.

Progression

We have saved a very important point for last—the old law of readiness. Your players must have proper instruction, and proper lead-up to the activity at hand. In other words, you must use the proper sequence and progression of skills in your sport. You do not take your football team on the field on the first day of practice and have them scrimmage—at least you shouldn't.

Progression through a sequence of skills is essential before your athletes are ready to scrimmage. But what is that sequence or progression? Again, you must know your sport. You will probably need to work on pitching, hitting, and fielding before you work on pick-off plays. You will probably have to work on shooting, dribbling, and passing before you put in your fast-break offense. You must determine those skills that are necessary and teach those skills before you start tackling, before you start a scrimmage, or before you let a gymnast try a maneuver without a spotter.

Because every sport activity is composed of subskills, you must take your players through the best sequence of subskills so that they are ready to perform the basic skill. For instance, to safely and competently pass block, you must know and teach your football players the sequence and progression of all the subskills. You need to plan your instruction so that none of your players attempts a skill for which he or she has inadequate background. Furthermore, you must appreciate the individual differences of your players and realize not all of them are going to master the subskills at the same time. It will take longer for some of your players to be ready than it will for others. Before attempting to perform a skill, your players must know the skill, have mastered the progressions required to perform the skill, and have no performance reservations.

RECOMMEN-DATIONS

1. Be very careful about deviating from approved plans, especially with a spur-of-the-moment decision.

2. Plans should be well-thought out, written, and retained.

3. Plans should be written in consideration of the players' performance.

4. Start your planning at the end and work forward to the beginning of your practice or season.

5. Allow time in your plan for repeated explanations of the risks of the sport.

6. Know your sport, be current in all facets of it, and include improvements in technique and conditioning in your plans.

7. Use the proper sequence and progression in teaching the subskills and skills of your sport. Be sure your players are ready to perform the skill before they attempt it.

Your best plans are only as good as your ability to implement them. Having a sound plan is no assurance you will not be negligent, but it is certainly an indication you have foresight and are aware of your responsibilities. Because of the nature of judicial scrutiny in recent court decisions, it is more imperative now than ever before that you plan carefully and are able to prove you have done so.

Chapter 4
Warning of Risks of Activities

WARNINGS

At the beginning of this guide, we described a couple of lawsuits in which coaches initially were found negligent because they did not sufficiently warn their players of the risks of an activity. These cases indicate the necessity of warning your players not only of the risks of the game, but also of any dangers they may face if they use improper, dangerous techniques. Also your players must know, understand, and appreciate the risks of an activity before they can assume those risks.

These three levels of comprehension—knowing, understanding, and appreciating are important and must be clarified. A one-time brief summary of the dangers within a sport is not sufficient warning to give to your players. Your warning should be thorough, clear, and repeated. If the sport is a contact or collision sport, it might be wise for you to give your players access to the warnings every day. Remember that the perception of risk is skill related, and a beginner does not have the same comprehension or appreciation as does an intermediate or expert player.

At some levels in football, for example, players are asked to read along with the coaches a prepared statement of the risks of the sport. The players then sign this statement, indicating they have read it and post it on the inside of their locker door so that every day when they open their lockers

to dress, they have the chance to see and be reminded of the risks inherent in the sport.

In order for your players to know, understand, and appreciate the risks of the sport, it is important that (a) they have a clear perception of the risks and potential for injury; (b) they clearly and fully perceive the nature and character of these risks and the possibility of injury; and (c) they be fully and sensitively aware of these risks and the extent of possible injury. For example, if your warning contains a reference to quadriplegia, be sure your players know what this term means. This is what the courts are asking you to provide your players.

INHERENT RISKS

The only risks your players may assume are those risks that are an inherent part of the sport. It is possible for them to assume the risk of a sprained ankle when playing basketball, but they should not assume the risk of running into a folded-up trampoline left at the edge of the basketball court.

A classic example of the distinction between the two types of risks occurred in a New York case (*Stevens v. Central School District No. 1 of the Town of Ramapo*, 1966). In this instance, an experienced adult player was playing basketball in a school gymnasium where he had played a number of times before. As he drove in for a lay-up, he was pushed out-of-bounds and toward the gymnasium door, which had a tiny window made of unreinforced glass. In bracing himself for the impact, one of the player's arms went through this small window, and he suffered severe lacerations to his arm. The gymnasium had been used for basketball for 16 years, and not once during those years had that window been broken. Furthermore, the building's architect testified that he felt it was not necessary for reinforced glass to be used in the facility. Nevertheless, the court found in favor of the injured player, noting that negligence occurred because the player was exposed to a risk beyond the scope of the game.

Changes in technique or equipment can cause a change in inherent risks. For example, the development of the Fosbury Flop surely caused a change in the inherent risks of high jumping; because athletes now land on their backs instead of their feet the risks of injury have increased. Another example is the development of glass panels which changed the inherent risks of racquetball and handball by making the ball and the wall harder to see.

Generally, an inherent risk is a risk incurred in a normal game played within the rules on a safe facility by trained players who have had qualified instruction and who know, understand, and appreciate the risks of the game. However, inherent risks sometimes do change, depending on improvement in different facets of the game. Two ski injury cases better illustrate this point. These lawsuits occurred approximately 20 years apart. In the latter case, the court stated that improvements in ski slope grooming techniques made the inherent risk in the earlier case unacceptable 20 years later.

Remember, your players can only assume those risks which are an inherent part of the sport, and you must do whatever you can to assure they know, understand, and appreciate those risks. Your language and technique for informing players of these risks must vary with the age and maturity of your players. The NCAA warning on football risks (which follows) is probably too complicated for Pop Warner players. Coaches working with younger players would need to simplify this warning in order for their players to acquire the same three-layered level of comprehension (knowing, understanding, and appreciating) about the risks of football.

EXAMPLES OF WARNINGS USED

NCAA Football Warning

Four examples of the types of warnings we feel are appropriate for various sports are illustrated in this section. The NCAA has formulated the following statement on the shared responsibility for sport safety for college football players:

SHARED RESPONSIBILITY FOR SPORT SAFETY

A Statement of the NCAA Committee on Competitive Safeguards and Medical Aspects of Sports

1. Serious head and neck injuries, leading to death, permanent brain damage, or quadriplegia (extensive paralysis from injury to the spinal cord at the neck level), occur each year in football. The toll is relatively small (less than one fatality for every 100,000 players, and an estimated one nonfatal severe brain and spinal cord injury for every 100,000 players), but persistent. They cannot be completely prevented due to the tremendous forces occasionally encountered in football collisions, but they can be minimized by manufacturer, coach, and player compliance with accepted safety standards.

2. The National Operating Commission on Standards for Athletic Equipment (NOCSAE) seal on a helmet indicates that a manufacturer has complied with the best available engineering standards for

head protection. By keeping a proper fit, by not modifying its design, and by reporting to the coach or equipment manager any need for its maintenance, the athlete is also complying with the purpose of the NOCSAE standard.

3. The rules against intentional butting, ramming, or spearing the opponent with the helmeted head are there to protect the helmeted person much more than the opponent being hit. The athlete who does not comply with these rules is the candidate for catastrophic injury. For example, no helmet can offer protection to the neck, and quadriplegia now occurs more frequently than brain damage. The typical scenario of this catastrophic injury in football is the lowering of one's head while making a tackle. The momentum of the body tries to bend the neck after the helmeted head is stopped by the impact, and the cervical spine cannot be "splinted" as well by the neck's muscles with the head lowered as with the preferred "face up, eyes forward, neck bulled" position. When the force at impact is sufficient, the vertebrae in the neck can dislocate or break, cause damage to the spinal cord they had been protecting, and thereby produce permanent loss of motor and sensory function below the level of injury.

4. Because of the impact forces in football, even the "face up" position is no guarantee against head or neck injury. Further, the intent to make contact "face up" is no guarantee that that position can be maintained at the moment of impact. Consequently, the teaching of blocking/tackling techniques which keep the helmeted head from receiving the brunt of the impact are now required by rule and coaching ethics, and coaching techniques which help athletes maintain or regain the "face up" position during the milieu of a play must be respected by the athletes.

For the sport of football, the NCAA encourages coaches to discuss this information with their squad at the onset of the season and to put a copy in each player's locker for additional emphasis. Coaches are then expected to remind their players of the essentials periodically during the season.

***King County
Schools'
Football Warning***

As another example in football, the high schools in King County, Washington, have formulated the following warning to parents and high-school-aged players as a result of the

$6,300,000 negligence award described in chapter 1 of this guide:

> I understand that the dangers and risks of playing or practicing to play tackle football include, but are not limited to, death, serious neck and spinal injuries which may result in complete or partial paralysis, brain damage, serious injury to virtually all internal organs, serious injury to virtually all bones, joints, ligaments, muscles, tendons, and other aspects of the muscular skeletal system, and serious injury or impairment to other aspects of my body and general health and well being.

Players and parents must sign this statement prior to the season.

Trampoline Warnings

The trampoline, once an endangered species, is being revived through the use of an improved teaching system and of clear warnings of the possibility of injury. The basic trampoline instructional program is now a non-somersaulting program. One of the basic instructional books on non-somersaulting trampolining contains two warnings on the inside of its cover (Harris, 1977). The first is a statement by the American Society for Testing and Materials, and the second refers to the potential dangers of somersaulting.

WARNING

1. Misuse and abuse of this trampoline is dangerous and can cause serious injuries.

2. Trampolines, being rebounding devices, propel the performer to unaccustomed heights and into a variety of body movements.

3. All purchasers and all persons using the trampoline must become familiar with the manufacturer's recommendations for the proper assembly, use, and care of the trampoline, as well as being alert to the performer's own limitations in the execution of trampoline skills. Assembly instructions, selected precautions, recommended instructional techniques and progressions, and suggestions for the care and maintenance of trampolines are included to promote safe, enjoyable use.

WARNING: CRIPPLING INJURIES CAN OCCUR DURING SOMERSAULTS!

Somersaulting should never be attempted without an overhead safety harness operated by a trained instructor. Refer to instruction manual. Almost all the benefits and enjoyment of the trampoline can be obtained by learning the non-somersaulting, twisting skills and routines provided in this manual.

Any activity involving motion or height creates the possibility of accidental injury. This equipment is intended for use *only* by properly trained and qualified participants under supervised conditions. Use without proper supervision could be *dangerous* and should *not* be undertaken or permitted. Before using, *know your own limitations* and the limitation of this equipment. If in doubt, always consult your instructor.

Always inspect for loose fittings or damage and test stability before each use.

Racquetball Warning

Racquetball is not a particularly hazardous sport, but we have constructed the following statement to be carefully read and signed prior to playing the sport:

WARNING FOR RACQUETBALL

Racquetball is a reasonably safe sport as long as certain guidelines are followed. It can develop aerobic and anaerobic fitness. It places physiological stresses on you comparable to basketball or handball. If you have any physical condition that precludes you from such activities, please obtain a physician's consent to participate and play with caution.

Eye injuries can occur in racquetball. For that reason, eyeguards are mandatory for this class. These are protective devices but cannot insure eye safety. *Do not look at a ball while it is being hit.* A racquetball can come off a racquet at speeds in excess of 120 miles per hour. *Turn your face away from all shots.*

WARNING FOR RACQUETBALL (Cont.)

Racquetball is played in a 20 x 20 x 40 court. Learn court presence (i.e., know where you are in relation to the walls and to your fellow competitor). Racquetball is not a collision sport, so don't make it one. Avoid crowding a fellow-competitor. Give him or her room for a complete swing, including follow through. *Be sure your wrist straps are always secure.*

It is perhaps inevitable that you will be hit by a ball. This is painful and will cause a bruise which should be iced as soon as possible. From our experience, if you are hit by a ball or racquet, it is generally *your* fault. Give each other room to play and shoot without contact.

Racquetball is a game of sudden stops or starts. We recommend wearing two pair of socks, cotton inner and woolen outer. *Use only court shoes. Do not use running shoes.* The higher soles of running shoes and sharper edges tend to produce ankle injuries.

When entering a court, always knock, and wait for the door to be opened from *within*.

Do you have any questions?

I have read the preceding and certify that I am physically fit for the racquetball class. I further attest that I have sufficient experience to enable me to participate in this class. I fully know, understand, and appreciate the risks inherent in the sport of racquetball. I am voluntarily participating in this activity.

_____ AGE _____ DATE_____
(Signature)

Using Warnings

These are all good examples of the warnings now necessary to give to your players. It is a good idea for you to carefully read through these warnings with your players and have them (and their parents if your players are minors) sign and date the statement. Be sure to solicit and answer all questions. Be sure to retain these signed and dated statements for your files. This is particularly true if you are coaching minors. *For legal reasons, minors retain the right to bring suit until a period of time, usually 1 to 3 years after they reach the age of majority.* It may be important for you to keep this information and any other records, especially injury reports, on hand for a long time.

WAIVERS AND RELEASES OF LIABILITY

Legal Validity of a Waiver

Some of you may not be concerned about providing warnings or about your other legal duties because you have all of your players and their parents sign a statement which releases you from any liability in the event of an injury. These statements are generally referred to as waivers or releases of liability. In law, they are known as exculpatory agreements. However, you should not rely too heavily on these waivers for protection for a number of reasons.

The basic effect of an exculpatory agreement is to relieve one party of all or a part of its responsibility to another. Courts have tended to carefully scrutinize these agreements for a variety of reasons, particularly because they may tend to create dangerous conditions. *Most courts will not allow a person to waive his or her rights in the event of negligence because it is against public policy.* While some exculpatory clauses have been upheld, they have usually been so upheld with very experienced adult performers participating in a hazardous sport.

Voiding an Exculpatory Clause

A number of factors make the value of exculpatory clauses questionable or even nonexistent. The first of these is very pertinent, particularly if you are coaching or teaching young

athletes. Because these exculpatory clauses are formal agreements between two parties, they are regarded as contracts. Minors cannot be held to a contract because they do not possess the necessary maturity to fully comprehend the essentials of the contract. Most American sports involve young athletes (minors), so this means that waivers and releases of liability have little value. You can have the parents sign them, and they can agree to waive their right to bring suit, assuming they are not minors and the other voiding elements of exculpatory clauses are not present. But, the minor cannot waive this right. He retains this right because he cannot validly sign a contract.

Even if your athletes are of legal age, you must be aware of the following factors which can void an exculpatory clause:

1. A strong public policy which prohibits such a clause.

2. One party being in a clearly dominant position, such as an employer-employee relationship.

3. The presence of any fraud or misrepresentation in the clause.

4. Any agreement which is signed under duress.

5. The clause being so ambiguous that the party does not know what is being signed.

6. The clause or the conditions it creates are unreasonable. These clauses will not protect coaches from wanton, intentional, or reckless misconduct.

7. The agreement is unreasonable.

8. The signature for such an agreement does not immediately follow the agreement.

For all these reasons, waivers and releases of liability must be used with great care. In the event of negligence, do not rely totally on them as a defense.

Successful Use of a Waiver

For those of you who teach or coach an activity in which an exculpatory agreement may be applicable, the following release was successfully used as a defense in a scuba diving case in which an adult in an advanced scuba diving class drowned in Puget Sound (*Hewitt v. Miller*, 1974). The court held that the failure of a diver to surface is an inherent risk of the sport of scuba diving, and that by signing the release, the young man acknowledged the possibility of his own death from this inherent danger.

SAFETY AFFIRMATION AND RELEASE
(Read carefully, then sign)

I, _____ , hereby affirm that I have previously completed a certified beginning course of instruction in SCUBA diving prior to enrolling in this course. By enrolling in this course I certify that I am cognizant of all of the inherent dangers of skindiving and SCUBA diving, and of the basic safety rules for underwater activities.

I understand that it is not the purpose of this course to teach safety rules nor is it the function of the instructors to serve as the guardians of my safety. I also understand that I am to furnish my own equipment and I am responsible for its safety and good operating condition regardless of where I obtain it.

I understand and agree that neither this class nor its owners, operators, agents, or instructors, including but not limited to _____ , _____ d/b/a/* _____ and other unnamed assistants, may be held liable in any way for any occurrence in connection with the advanced SCUBA diving class which may result in injury, death, or other damages to me or my family, heirs, or assigns, and in consideration of being allowed to enroll in this course. I hereby personally assume all risks in connection with said course, and I further release the aforementioned instructors, program, agents and operators, including, but not limited to the persons mentioned, for any harm, injury, or damage which may befall me while I am enrolled as a student of the school, including all risks connected therewith, whether foreseen or unforeseen, and further to save and hold harmless said program and persons from any claim by me, or my family, estate, heirs, or assigns, arising out of my enrollment and participation in this course.

I further state that I am of lawful age and legally competent to sign this affirmation and release; that I understand the terms herein are contractual and not a mere recital; and that I have signed this document as my own free act.

I HAVE FULLY INFORMED MYSELF OF THE CONTENT OF THIS AFFIRMATION AND RELEASE BY READING IT BEFORE I SIGNED IT. I have had a medical examination to assure myself, and assume

```
┌──────────────────────────────────────────┐
│   SAFETY AFFIRMATION AND RELEASE (Cont.)   │
│                                            │
│   my own responsibility of physical        │
│   fitness and ca-                           │
│   pability to perform under the normal      │
│   conditions of                             │
│   an advanced diving program, and am        │
│   physically fit                            │
│   as attested to by the aforementioned     │
│   medical                                   │
│   examination.                              │
│                                            │
│   _____      _____      │
│   Signature                Date            │
│                                            │
└──────────────────────────────────────────┘
```

*d/b/a = doing business as

INFORMED CONSENT

Informed consent is a topic of increasing interest related to warnings. *Essentially, consent that is not informed is not consent at all.* If you are working in programs involving physical fitness testing or prescriptive exercise programs, it is a good idea for you to follow these six guidelines to obtain informed consent.

1. Inform the exercise program participant of the testing procedure and explain its purpose. This explanation should be thorough and unbiased.

2. Inform the participant of the risks and discomfort involved in these exercises and procedures.

3. Inform the participant of the benefits expected from the exercises or procedures.

4. Inform the participant of any alternative programs or tests that might be more advantageous for him or her.

5. Solicit questions regarding the testing procedures or exercise programs and give unbiased answers to these inquiries.

6. Inform the participant that he or she is free at any time to withdraw consent and discontinue participation without prejudice.

For such programs use a form like the following developed for the University of Montana Health and Fitness program, a voluntary program in the Department of Health and Physical Education serving the university's faculty and staff. This form was finally deemed acceptable after undergoing three draft revisions with the university legal counsel.

INITIAL FITNESS TESTING, PROGRAM PARTICIPATION, AND INFORMED CONSENT

The University of Montana Health and Fitness Program is a voluntary program available to members of the faculty and staff. The program will provide an opportunity for all employees to learn about—and pursue—a healthier lifestyle.

As part of a basic fitness evaluation, the University of Montana Health and Fitness Program administers a physical work capacity test, using the bicycle ergometer. This test is preceded with appropriate risk factor information. This includes a medical history and physical activity readiness questionnaire and a computerized health risk appraisal, designed to identify personal health risks. Resting heart rate and blood pressure measurements, and a resting electrocardiogram will also begin at a level you can easily accomplish and will be advanced in stages, depending upon your current level of fitness. We may stop the test at any time because of signs of fatigue or discomfort. Results obtained from this physical work capacity test will provide information necessary for the construction of an individualized exercise program. Questions pertaining to procedures used in the test, or results of the testing, are welcome.

There exists the possibility of certain changes occurring during the testing. They include abnormal blood pressure or heart rate response, fainting and disorders of the heart. Every effort will be made to minimize them through the use of the preliminary examination and observations during the testing. Emergency procedures have been developed, and trained personnel are available to deal with unusual situations which may arise.

After reading the preceding information, completing all the forms to the best of my ability, and having had any and all questions answered to my satisfaction, I certify that I am sufficiently fit to attempt the test and program and agree to participate with a full knowledge, understanding, and appreciation of the risks herein. I recognize the risks of illness and injury inherent in any exercise program and am participating upon the express agreement and under-

INITIAL FITNESS TESTING,
PROGRAM PARTICIPATION,
AND INFORMED CONSENT (Cont.)

standing that I, for myself, my heirs, and executors, hereby waive and release the University of Montana, the Department of Health and Physical Education, and the University of Montana Health and Fitness Program and all their agents from and against any and all claims, costs, liabilities, expenses, or judgments, and hereby agree to indemnify and hold harmless the University of Montana, the Department of Health and Physical Education, and the University Health and Fitness Program from and against any and all claims, damages, liabilities or causes of action, except for illness and injury directly resulting from gross negligence or wilful misconduct.

_____   _____
Signature   Witness

_____   _____
Date   Date

RECOMMEN-DATIONS

1. Warn your players of the inherent risks of the game, and of the dangers they face if they use improper, dangerous techniques. Be sure your warnings enable your players to know, understand, and appreciate the risks of the activity.

2. Put your warnings in written form and be sure they are carefully read and signed. Retain a copy of this signed form for your files. If you deem it necessary, give your players an additional copy which they can place in a location where it will be frequently seen.

3. After presenting the warnings, be sure to ask for questions, giving thorough and unbiased answers to these questions.

4. Remind your players frequently and regularly of the risks of the activity.

5. Be sure your warnings are clear and comprehensive. Be sure they are written in a language your players will understand.

6. Remember that inherent risks can change because of changing techniques or equipment in your sport.

7. Be leery of relying on waivers or releases of liability

as a defense against negligence, especially if your participants are minors.

8. If necessary, be sure to obtain the informed consent of the participants in your program.

Because one of your defenses in the event of a negligence lawsuit may be assumption of risk, you must do all you can to be sure that your participants know, understand, and appreciate these risks, and that they are subjected only to the inherent risks of the activity.

Many risks that are not inherent are created by poor facilities or equipment. Providing a safe environment is the topic of the next chapter.

Chapter 5
Providing a Safe Environment

RECOGNIZING HAZARDS

Many lawsuits in sport contain an allegation of an unsafe area or unsafe equipment. This is not surprising when you consider the varied areas and the wide variety of equipment used in sport. It is your responsibility to provide your players with as safe a facility as possible and with good equipment in proper condition.

ACTUAL AND CONSTRUCTIVE NOTICE

Some hazards are easily recognizable. You are responsible for eliminating them to the extent you can or for informing your supervisor of the condition and the necessity of having them repaired or removed. Doing this is called *actual notice.*

If you should have known of a particular condition, there may be *constructive notice.* In essence, this means you are responsible for what a reasonable and a prudent coach should have noticed, whether you did or not. This was a critical fac-

tor in a Louisiana lawsuit, in which the court found school authorities to be negligent (*Ardoin et al. v. Evangeline Parish School Board*, 1979). In this case, a young boy playing softball during physical education class fell and injured his right knee when running from second to third base. The boy tripped on a piece of concrete imbedded in the ground near the basepath. The court held that the school authorities had constructive knowledge of this condition and should have anticipated and discovered the potential danger, eliminating the slab before allowing students to use the field.

You are not an insurer of safety, but you must provide and maintain facilities relatively free from injury-producing conditions. Do not allow the facility or the equipment used to create risks which are not an inherent part of the activity. *Because you are responsible for the immediate supervision of your coaching area, most of the responsibility for keeping the area safe is yours.* It is your duty to inspect the area regularly and thoroughly, to warn your players of any hazards (especially hidden hazards or hazards caused by changing conditions), and to make recommendations to your supervisors to remedy such hazards or to provide protective equipment for those hazards that cannot be removed.

FACILITIES

Listing all the facility conditions that have caused negligence would take too much space. This may not just involve the playing area, but such facilities as the locker room or shower room. All of the areas you supervise, generally or specifically, need to be as safe as possible.

Four basic reasons for lawsuits involving facilities are unacceptable risks of injury, poor maintenance, improper design, and defective equipment.

Risks Exist

An inherent risk of injury exists in any facility when participating in sport. You need to reduce this risk as much as possible, but accept that it is impossible to entirely eliminate all risks from sport.

Poor Maintenance

If the facility is inadequately maintained, the chances of injury are increased. You may need to explain to the maintenance personnel the requirements of your sport and the type of care the facility needs.

Improper Design

A facility must be designed and constructed with great care. In one community, parents built neighborhood playgrounds at various schools. At one of these sites, the school's insurance company requested the removal of a climbing bar and horizontal ladder because it was too high, creating too much risk for the children (and for the insurance company).

Defective Equipment

In 1981, a New York lawsuit involved defective facility equipment. A man grabbed a railing on a platform in the gymnasium, the railing gave way, and the man fell to his death (*Woodring v. Board of Education of Manhasset*, 1981). The court held that, among other things, the construction of the railing and posts and the manner in which the railing was secured were not in accordance with proper construction practice and should have been discovered by an adequate inspection. An award was made against the school district for $1,400,000.

MAKING THE FACILITY SAFER

Check Standards

You can do a number of things to provide your players with a safe facility. The first is to make sure that the proper standards are applied. We have an area at the University of Montana that violates a number of standards and, consequently, is not used as much as it could be. This area has a basketball court at least 125 feet long, has very poor lighting, and has backgrounds which, when combined with questionable lighting, make certain activities dangerous. In addition, sharp edges and rails are too close to the playing areas. Nothing can be done about the area because it is part of the basketball arena used for seating. But because of its design, its use is limited.

If you were coaching tennis in this facility (it is designed as an indoor tennis court), you would notice that the background for tennis is beige, and that white or dirty white tennis balls coming out of a beige background with poor lighting could be dangerous. In addition, the distance between the tennis playing surface and the railing on one side and the fold-up bleachers on the other is inadequate. Your players would need to be warned and protected from running into these objects.

Regular Inspections

You need to inspect your facility carefully to be sure it is safe for your activity. Courts have consistently held that these inspections need to be regular and thorough. How regular and thorough depends on the facility and the activity, but at the

very minimum, you should inspect your facility at the beginning and end of each sport or unit of instruction. If your sport is a dangerous one, this inspection might be necessary every day, or even every time the facility or equipment is used.

Your inspection needs to be thorough enough so that you notice what a reasonable and a prudent coach or physical education teacher should have noticed. For example, in one playground a slide was inspected every week, but because the inspection failed to reveal a loose and protruding bolt upon which a girl cut her hand, the inspection was not thorough enough. Another factor in the court's judgment in the case where the man was killed when a railing collapsed was that a nut and bolt to hold the railing in place was not secure, and that the school district had no program of preventive maintenance or inspection of the facilities in the gymnasium. Therefore, be sure to inspect your facility and the equipment you use regularly and thoroughly. The more dangerous the activity, the more regular and thorough your inspection must be.

Facility Rules

You should also give precise rules for the use of a facility and enforce these rules, which should include instructions for you and your players in the event of an emergency. For example, in case of a fire, your players must know which exit to use and what procedures to follow.

In your facility, remove items or pieces of equipment that are not going to be used. If they are dangerous items and attractive to your participants, make them inaccessible by *locking them away.* For example, it is dangerous to leave an open trampoline close to your basketball practice area. Its mere presence can be dangerous to the players practicing basketball, but it also invites your players to use it. A somersaulting injury on a trampoline is not an inherent risk of the sport of basketball!

Try to become aware of sport-specific conditions that might make your facility more dangerous than it should be. For example, if your lighting and background colors are poor for basketball, it may be necessary for you to warn your players about this condition and perhaps use a multicolored ball like the one used by the old American Basketball Association.

Preventive Maintenance

You can help provide a safer facility in two other ways. The first, *preventive maintenance*, simply means your inspections should lead to maintenance of the facility adequate to prevent accidents from happening in the facility.

Shared Responsibility

Shared responsibility is the other way you can provide a safer facility. Teach your assistants, your players, the custodians, other coaches, your trainer, and your other helpers to look for potentially dangerous conditions in your facility. Doing this will help prove you have given your duty of providing a safe facility due consideration. Shared responsibility will also result in more thorough inspections of your facility and, thus, a safer facility.

EQUIPMENT

Much of what has been said about providing a safe facility applies equally to the equipment used when you coach your sport. Many lawsuits involve poor or improper equipment. You are responsible for providing the best equipment you can

afford for your players. A study of a youth football program revealed that the equipment was given out on a first-come, first-served basis. The result was that some young players received helmets which were either too large or too small. In some instances, the players had removed the webbing from the helmet and wore just the plastic shell when they played. Some of the players who received helmets too large for them stuffed those helmets with newspaper for better fit. Unfortunately, newspaper is not suitable protective padding for the inside of a football helmet.

Improper Use of Sports Equipment

Equipment does not become a factor only in contact or dangerous sports as shown in a Pennsylvania case some time ago (*Styer v. Reading*, 1948). The participants were children in a summer recreation program on a school playground and in a small room in the basement of the school. This room was poorly lighted and had a variety of unstored equipment lying about, including badminton equipment. Badminton is not a very dangerous sport; however, the room was dark, the play was not properly supervised, and the shuttlecock (an outdoor one) had a hard rubber tip. Two of the children were batting this shuttlecock around awhile without a net; as one girl said she was quitting, the other took one last shot, accidentally striking the other girl in the eye. The eye had to be removed after several operations. The young girl was awarded $16,000.

This case provides a good example of what can happen, even in a safe activity, if equipment is used improperly. You must provide adequate equipment and use it properly in a safe facility. In addition, you also have other equipment responsibilities.

Quality Control

The first of these other responsibilities is to select your equipment carefully. Use reputable dealers and choose the best equipment affordable. You must be knowledgeable about the equipment used in your sport and keep abreast of changes. Be aware of the kinds of equipment involved in common injuries affecting athletes in your sport.

Furthermore, make sure your equipment meets the *standards* for that equipment, should such standards exist. If you are coaching handball, for example, be sure your eyeguards meet the American Society for Testing and Materials standards. If you are coaching football, be sure your helmets meet the National Operating Committee on Safety in Athletic Equipment (NOCSAE) standards.

If it is necessary for you to install, fit, or adjust equipment, be sure you do so correctly. Ski equipment requires maintenance and adjustment by a trained expert. If you are not able to fit face masks onto football helmets, have someone do it who knows how or have that person show you the correct procedure. The same applies if your equipment needs repair.

If the equipment is protective equipment, be sure that those who repair it know what they are doing. Some equipment needs to be periodically reconditioned. Football helmets are generally considered to be in need of reconditioning after 3 or 4 years of use. Again, rely on reputable reconditioners and be sure that any standards set for your equipment are met, especially for dangerous equipment or protective equipment.

Warning Your Players

Be sure you present the necessary warnings to your players regarding the use of equipment. Warning labels are now attached to more and more sports equipment (e.g., football helmets, trampolines, motorcycle helmets). If your equipment has a warning concerning proper use and limitations, you must interpret this warning so your players know, understand, and appreciate the dangers. As an example, the National Operating Committee on Standards for Athletic Equipment warning on football helmets reads:

WARNING

Do not use this helmet to butt, ram or spear an opposing player. This is in violation of the football rules and such use can result in severe head or neck injury, paralysis or death to you and possible injury to your opponent. No helmet can prevent all head or neck injuries a player might receive while participating in football.

Do not assume your players have read this warning. Instead, go over the warning with them, showing them where it's written on their helmets. Explain the dangers of football, and explain the proper use of the helmet when playing football. Even the best helmet with the most explicit warning is useless if you continue to teach or encourage the improper use of that helmet.

Furthermore, do not create a warranty for a product when the manufacturer has not provided such a warranty. Do not tell your players that a piece of equipment can do something it cannot. Do not, for example, tell your racquetball players that eyeguards prevent eye injuries because they don't: They do reduce the likelihood and the severity of eye injuries, but they do not prevent them. Similarly, do not tell skiers that certain ski bindings will prevent injuries.

Finally, remember to inspect your equipment regularly and thoroughly. Try to get others to share this responsibility as well. Some pieces of protective equipment include a checklist of items to be examined prior to each use. If your players are doing this inspection, be sure they do so correctly.

Changes in Equipment Standards

Keep current with the causes of injury and with equipment improvements by reading the professional literature in your sport. This will help you avoid having your players use an outmoded or dangerous piece of equipment. For example, a few years ago, some football helmets appeared with a soft rubber padding on the outside. They were used for a few years and then removed from the market because the manufacturers felt that this protective padding created more friction and actually increased the likelihood of an injury. You need to be aware of changes such as this in equipment design and use in your sport. If your equipment, thought to be safe at the time of purchase, is now considered unsafe or questionable, do not use it.

PRODUCTS LIABILITY

Products liability is the liability of a manufacturer for producing a defective product. It may seem that this should not be a matter of great concern to you, but it is for at least two reasons. First, coaches are involved in a number of products liability suits as co-defendants. This involvement is more likely if a coach is connected with the manufacturing, selling, fitting, advertising, or representing of a product.

Second, one of the effects of products liability suits is that the cost of liability insurance and of the lawsuit is passed on to the consumer, resulting in higher prices for your athletic equipment. Indeed, some experts feel that the threat of products liability suits may result in the elimination of some sports at the public school level. In his excellent book, *The Death of an American Game*, John Underwood (1979) feels this is a possibility with football because of the increase in serious injuries and costs.

In some cases, the nature and techniques of a sport are changed by these suits. The elimination of spearing in football and the development of non-somersaulting trampolining are two examples. Again, you must stay current with these changes in your sport, including those brought about by these products liability suits.

Manufacturers of sporting goods equipment are endeavoring to meet the demands of the courts by doing all they can to produce good products. This means that closer judicial scrutiny will be on coaching methods and techniques.

RECOMMEN- DATIONS

Because the concerns about facilities and equipment are interrelated, both have been considered in this chapter. Much more could be said about each, but this is designed to be a legal guide, not an explicit set of standards applicable to all coaches. You should, however, consider all of the following in providing a safe facility and good equipment:

1. You have the duty to notice and remedy hazardous conditions in your facility. This duty means that you should notice what a reasonable and a prudent coach would notice.

2. Inspect the facility regularly and thoroughly, at least at the beginning and end of a season or unit of instruction.

3. Change any dangerous conditions you can, provide protective equipment for those you cannot, and put your superiors on notice through a written recommendation about correcting or improving a dangerous condition.

4. Be sure that any standards applicable to your sport are met by your facility and your equipment.

5. Give precise rules for the use of an area. Be sure to include any rules for emergencies.

6. If a piece of equipment is not going to be used, it should be out of the way. If it is a dangerous piece of equipment, it should be inaccessible when it is not being used.

7. Become aware of sport-specific conditions that might make your facility more dangerous than it should be.

8. Work with everyone in your program to develop and to implement the concepts of preventive maintenance and shared responsibility.

9. Buy the best equipment you can afford from reputable dealers.

10. Be aware of changes in equipment used in your sport. Be alert for any piece of equipment in your sport that is associated with a high rate of injury.

11. Allow only those who are trained to install, fit, adjust, repair, or recondition equipment.

12. Present the necessary warnings to your players for the use of the equipment. Be sure they know, understand, and appreciate these warnings.

13. Inspect your equipment regularly and thoroughly. The more dangerous the equipment, or the more protective it is designed to be, the more regularly and thoroughly you and others should carry out these inspections.

14. Teach the proper technique along with the proper use of the equipment.

15. Do not tell your players that a piece of equipment can do something it cannot do.

16. Realize that products liability suits involve and concern you, and that the courts are more likely to legally

scrutinize your behavior because manufacturers are better meeting the demands of the courts in the production of sports equipment.

It is impossible to design a completely safe facility, and it is probably impossible to develop completely safe equipment. Nevertheless, it is up to you to provide the best equipment and the safest facility you can for your players, exposing them only to the inherent risks of a sport.

Chapter 6
Evaluating Players for Injury or Incapacity

PERFORMING SAFELY

Don't let the title of this chapter mislead you. You are not responsible for conducting complete examinations of your players prior to play, but you have a duty to make sure your players are ready physically to perform safely. Use family and team physicians, athletic trainers, nurses, parents, and your own good judgment to determine if a player has a potential injury or incapacitating condition which may preclude play.

CASE EXAMPLES

CASE 1: In 1966 a young girl was injured in a physical education class in Oregon (*Summers v. Milwaukie Union High School District No. 5*, 1971). Jumping 14 inches high from an elevated board which rested on a coiled spring, she touched her toes in the air, landed on her feet, lost her balance, and fell backward. She suffered a compression fracture of two vertebrae. The young girl already had a history of back trouble and had frequently consulted with a physician for advice. The

physician requested from the school a list of exercises and a description of the type of gymnastics the girl was to perform at school. This request was made of the school at least four different times, the last being about 1 week prior to the accident. The list was never provided. The girl's physician testified that she should not have been doing the springboard exercise, and had he known she was doing so, he would have recommended that she not participate in that exercise. The girl was awarded damages. The court held that the school district's failure to furnish the requested list of exercises was negligent behavior, for if the school district had done so, the girl would not have performed the exercise. In its discussion, the court indicated that this was a good example of the failure of the duty of constructive notice. Constructive notice means "A person is bound not only by what he knows but also by what he might have known had he exercised ordinary diligence."

CASE 2: A famous California case describes another facet of this duty. A young girl took a tumbling class rather than the gymnasium class she had wanted (*Bellman v. San Francisco High School District*, 1938). In this class the students had 18 exercises they could perform, and to get a passing grade had to complete 10 of the 18 exercises. One of the exercises, called the "roll over two," required the student to jump over two students lying on the floor, land on her hands, and do a forward roll to a standing position. This "roll over two" was not, however, a required exercise.

The girl had expressed strong reservations about performing this exercise, which was the only one that required the students to have their bodies completely off the floor for a portion of the time. During the course of the class, the reluctant girl finally indicated to the instructor that she was ready to try. She attempted the exercise but landed incorrectly and suffered a head injury. Despite a vigorous dissent, the court found the school to have been negligent, stating that the school's employees knew or should have known that because of the girl's mental or physical condition, she was not ready for this activity. This case caused a great deal of concern for coaches and physical educators because of its emphasis on assessing the mental readiness of participants to perform.

CONSIDER-ATIONS

Physical Examinations

Most texts on the organization and administration of sport and physical education recommend that your players have a regular physical examination prior to practice or play. The nature of this physical examination has changed, or at least we hope it has. In the past if a player had a pulse, blood pressure, and could cough at the appropriate time, he was deemed ready for action. Hopefully, the physical examination you obtain for your athletes is a bit more stringent. States and state organizations differ on their recommendations about the regularity of thorough physical examinations. Some state organizations require a thorough annual physical examination. Others believe that children need less frequent examinations. You must check which policy applies to your sport organization.

The University of Washington School of Medicine has prepared a list of disqualifying conditions for sports participation from the American Medical Association publication, *Medical Evaluation of the Athlete—A Guide.* The chart is included on p. 54 to give you an idea of the conditions that may preclude an athlete from participating. Note the interesting categorizations of sport: Collision, Contact, Noncontact, and Other. The authors of the chart emphasize that in practice each patient should be judged on an individual basis in conjunction with his or her cardiologist and operating surgeon.

DISQUALIFYING CONDITIONS FOR SPORTS PARTICIPATION

	Collision[1]	Contact[2]	Noncontact[3]	Other[4]
General				
Acute infections: respiratory, genitourinary, infectious mononucleosis, hepatitis, active rheumatic fever, active tuberculosis	x	x	x	x
Obvious physical immaturity in comparison with other competitors	x	x		
Hemorrhagic disease: hemophilia, purpura, and other serious bleeding tendencies	x	x	x	x
Diabetes, inadequately controlled	x	x	x	x
Diabetes, controlled				
Jaundice	x	x	x	x
Eyes				
Absence or loss of function of one eye	x	x		
Respiratory				
Tuberculosis (active or symptomatic)	x	x	x	x
Severe pulmonary insufficiency	x	x	x	x
Cardiovascular				
Mitral stenosis, aortic stenosis, aortic insufficiency, coarctation of aorta, cyanotic heart disease, recent carditis of any etiology	x	x	x	x
Hypertension on organic basis	x	x	x	x
Previous heart surgery for congenital or acquired heart disease				
Liver				
Enlarged liver	x	x		
Skin				
Boils, impetigo, and herpes simplex gladiatorum	x	x		
Spleen				
Enlarged spleen	x	x		
Hernia				
Inguinal or femoral hernia	x	x	x	
Musculoskeletal				
Symptomatic abnormalities or inflammations	x	x	x	x
Functional inadequacy of the musculoskeletal system, congenital or acquired, incompatible with the contact or skill demands of the sport	x	x	x	
Neurological				
History or symptoms of previous serious head trauma, or repeated concussion	x			
Controlled convulsive disorder				
Convulsive disorder not moderately well controlled by medication	x			
Previous surgery on head	x	x		
Renal				
Absence of one kidney	x	x		
Renal disease	x	x	x	x
Genitalia				
Absence of one testicle, undescended testicle				

Note. From *Medicine* (1978, Fall), University of Washington School of Medicine, **5**(3), p. 6. Reprinted with permission of the American Medical Association from the *Medical Evaluation of the Athlete—A Guide*, September, 1977, Chicago: American Medical Association.

[1]Football, rugby, hockey, lacrosse, etc.; [2]baseball, soccer, basketball, wrestling, etc.; [3]cross-country, track, tennis, crew, swimming, etc.; [4]bowling, golf, archery, field events, etc.

Readiness to Perform

You have a duty to exercise considerable care in identifying injuries and incapacitating conditions during the course of practice and play. When you observe these conditions, you may need to temporarily adjust a player's participation.

Then you have the problem of knowing when a player is ready to return to action following an injury. Seek help to solve this problem from the athlete's physician, the trainer, a school nurse, and the parents. Be very careful about permitting an athlete to return to play too soon after an injury. In carrying out this duty, it is certainly better to err on the conservative side rather than aggravate an injury by returning the athlete to action too soon.

Furthermore, you must not use any subtle pressure or coercion to intimidate the athlete to return to play. If an athlete truly does not want to resume play, or if he or she has valid reservations about returning to action, do not force him or her to play. This is true even if the injury has apparently healed.

You also need to be aware that injuries and some incapacitating conditions are dynamic; they may improve, then get worse. In addition, injuries and incapacitating conditions affect play more in some areas than in others, and in some parts of activities more than in others. You should be flexible enough not to stereotype athletes as perpetually injured or as hypochondriacs; instead, consult with them, talk to them, and be sure they are ready to perform.

Two other factors may affect your coaching with regard to injuries and incapacitating conditions. Both of these are concerns because of recent federal laws and apply more to school sports and physical education programs than nonschool programs. But they should be considered by all coaches.

Education for All Handicapped Children Act 1975

School coaches need to pay greater attention to allowing handicapped children to participate as much as possible. The Education for All Handicapped Children Act is designed to assure that all handicapped children have a free, appropriate public education available to them. An essential part of this law is called "mainstreaming," which requires that these students be given a regular educational experience whenever possible. Interestingly, instruction in physical education is the only curricular area included in this law's description of special education. Furthermore, this law asks that extracurricular services and activities be provided so handicapped children have an equal opportunity for participation in such activities.

This act poses two problems for school coaches: The first is the safety of the handicapped participants when playing with nonhandicapped persons; the second is the safety of the nonhandicapped persons. For example, if a participant has a prosthesis (an artificial limb) and wants to play in a contact sport, what must you do to enhance this player's safe participation and also the safety of the other players? At this point, we cannot give you explicit guidelines. You must do what you judge to be best, but still be sensitive to a handicapped person's right to participate.

Recently, several students have won the right to play in sports from which they were previously excluded because of handicapping conditions. You must be more alert to the implications of this law for your program, when applicable.

Child Abuse Prevention and Treatment Act 1974

The other federal law of which you need to be aware is called the Child Abuse Prevention and Treatment Act. This law requires certain professionals who know or have reasonable cause to suspect that a child, known to them in their professional or official capacity, is an abused or neglected child, to report the matter promptly to the department of social and rehabilitation services. A wide list of professionals have this duty, including school teachers and coaches, other school officials, and employees who work during regular school hours.

The law asks you to collect evidence and to submit a formal report. It is especially important that coaches and physical education teachers be aware of this law. Two of the signs of child abuse or neglect are lethargy in play and obvious bruises. Because you have a better chance to see more of the body in sports and physical education and because you should be able to detect lethargy in play, an awareness of this law, its requirements, and of local policies and procedures for reporting suspected child abuse is essential for today's coach.

Medical History

Finally, we recommend that you keep a record of the medical history of your participants. We have included the following form as a guide in drafting a form that is appropriate for you and your program. Keep these forms and update them whenever necessary. Use them in assessing the appropriateness of an activity for your participants.

ATHLETE MEDICAL HISTORY

Name_____ Date of birth _____

Address _____ Telephone _____

Parents_____ Emergency telephone_____

Physician_____ Physician's phone _____

Coach _____ Sport _____

History:

☐ (1) Immunizations, year of last tetanus booster _____

☐ (2) Last dentist visit _____

☐ (3) Handedness (left or right) _____

☐ (4) Allergies _____

☐ (5) Any medications, medicines, drugs now being taken _____
       _____

☐ (6) Heart: Murmur? Heart disease? Palpitation? Anyone under 50 years old in family die of heart
       problems?_____

☐ (7) Do you have to stop when running a half-mile, twice around the track? Asthma? Wheezing?
       Hay fever? _____

☐ (8) Have you ever been unconscious or knocked out (concussion)? _____

☐ (9) Have you ever had any trouble with
           Eyes (vision) _____
           Ears (hearing) _____
           Kidneys (urine)_____
           Hernias _____
           Testicles _____

☐ (10) Female menstrual history _____ x _____ x _____

☐ (11) Major medical illnesses (e.g., seizures, anemia, diabetes, arthritis, thyroid disease, bleeding
        disorders, hepatitis) _____

☐ (12) Overnight hospitalizations_____

☐ (13) Operations or surgery _____

☐ (14) Fractures or broken bones _____

☐ (15) Ever have a cast, splint, sling, cane, or crutches?_____

☐ (16) Ever have an x-ray of any bone or joint? _____

☐ (17) Ever have an injury that caused you to miss a game or practice?_____

Additional History Information

_____

_____

_____

History taken by (name)_____

RECOMMEN-DATIONS

1. Rely on family and team physicians, athletic trainers, school nurses, parents, and your good judgment in determining whether or not to permit injured players to participate.

2. A thorough yearly physical examination by a physician is strongly recommended for all your players.

3. Consider the mental state of your players. Never force or coerce players to participate if they have valid reservations about doing so.

4. Be judicious in allowing a player to return to action following an injury.

5. Remember that injuries are dynamic, and avoid stereotyping your players.

6. If applicable, follow the dictates of the Education for All Handicapped Children Act, and the Child Abuse Prevention and Treatment Act.

7. Keep a record of the medical history of your participants, update it, and use it for choosing appropriate activities.

Chapter 7
Matching and Equating Participants

MISMATCHES You have a duty not to allow your participants to be mismatched when playing your sport. A number of sport lawsuits have used size, weight, or age discrepancies as the basis for claiming negligence. In addition to these factors, others need to be considered. Recent changes in federal law have substantially revised the way in which you must fulfill this duty.

In essence, you must be absolutely certain that your players are not put at a serious disadvantage by the manner in which you have matched or equated them for competition. In the past, the common practice was to use convenient methods for setting up practices, scrimmages, or competitions. These practices may still be used, but not as casually as before, and not without some thought beforehand about the matches which may occur.

One court case ruled that even the scheduling of a game may create a mismatch: "It is possible that two football teams may be so disparate in size and ability that those responsi-

ble for supervising the athletic program would violate their duty in permitting the teams to play" (*Vendrell v. School District No. 26C Malheur County*, 1961). In 1983, a Chicago high school was so concerned about mismatches, it forfeited its entire schedule before the season began.

Georgia Tech once beat Cumberland College in a football game 222-0. Supposedly, this would be an example of such a mismatch. Unfortunately, no simple formulae which you can use to determine a mismatch exist. Instead, the courts ask you to consider a number of factors to assure the safety of your players.

We have identified at least eight different factors you should consider when matching players for practices or competitive situations which we will discuss in order of approximate priority. This order, however, will not be appropriate for certain sports and certain players. Ideally, you should consider all of these factors as you set up competitions for your players.

Before we discuss these factors in detail, remember that mismatches may occur in any activity. Even such relatively innocuous games as line soccer and touch football have produced mismatches. Although the possibility of a mismatch is more likely to have serious consequences in collision or contact sports, every activity demands that you pay some attention to equitably matching players for competition.

MATCHING FACTORS

Skill

The most important factor to consider in matching players is the *skill* each possesses. Your players should have a comparable degree of readiness to perform the skill. They should know and understand the techniques to be performed at about the same level. For example, you should not permit a highly skilled wrestler to wrestle a novice, even if all of the other factors mentioned in this chapter are equal. The advantage the skilled player has in the refinements and nuances of technique place the less skilled player at too severe a disadvantage.

In addition, your assessment of the skill of each player should, as much as possible, be objective. This is extremely difficult to accomplish because many sport skills do not lend themselves to objectivity. You must do more than just rely on hunches or select a method of matching which is merely convenient. If objectivity is difficult, obtain second and third opinions from other coaches.

Having a better player help a less skilled player is certainly a possibility, but be careful about having the two compete. Again, if a player has a valid reservation about a match you have arranged, do not use any coercion and do not embarrass the player into performing.

You also should consider the type of skill being performed. It is easier to be objective and to match players in a *closed skill* than in an *open skill*. Closed skills are those performed by the player with little or no reliance on another player. Golf and bowling are basically closed skills. Even in these sports, a mismatch is possible. The embarrassment, the frustration, the anxiety of having your weakest golfer play with your best golfer may not lead to a lawsuit, but it may so discourage your poorer golfer that his or her improvement and desire to continue is destroyed. Players performing in open skills, those performed with or against others, however, are more difficult to match because there is direct competition and less objectivity. If the sport you coach is an open skill sport, supervise it with greater caution.

Experience

When matching players, you must also consider their *experience*. Although skill and experience are somewhat related, experience includes some additional concerns.

Having two players compete against one another is dangerous if one has far greater experience in the sport. This poses a problem when you have a rapidly improving newcomer to the sport who has the potential to be an outstanding player, and you want to speed up his or her improvement by matching the athlete with a player who has far more experience. Again, your experienced player is going to have the advantage of knowing the subtleties of play during competitive conditions. Furthermore, competitive conditions create more tension and a greater flow of adrenalin. The experienced player may want to show up the newcomer. The newcomer may be more nervous, try too hard, and disrupt his or her normal skill.

We are not saying you cannot match players of varied experience: We are saying you should be careful when you do it. Observe the action closely, and watch for any danger signs during the course of play. If you sense the competition is not matched right, if you see the experienced player trying to show up the less experienced player, or if you see the less experienced player is not performing well, stop the competition. Needless to say, this is a difficult duty for you to carry out, and it requires your strict attention and concentration.

Injuries or Incapacitating Conditions

A third factor, the subject of our preceding chapter, is to consider the effect of any *injuries* or *incapacitating conditions* when matching your players. Follow the guidelines we mentioned in chapter 6.

Instruct your players to inform you of any injuries or conditions they have which might disrupt their performance. Some of these conditions which may cause you to reduce or eliminate competition are easily noticed, but it is impossible for you to sense headaches, backaches, colds, or mental states which might temporarily create a mismatch. Be sure that your players feel free to inform you of such conditions without being branded a sissy, a malingerer, or a hypochondriac. Be sensitive to the conditions of your players, especially those conditions that are not easily observable.

Maturity

Consider, also, the *maturity* of your players. Notice this factor is listed before height, weight, and age. The reason is because in certain age groups, maturity varies so much that these other factors are of secondary importance. It is quite possible for two 14-year-olds to be the same height and weight, but possess such a great difference in physical, emotional, and mental maturity that having these players compete against each other would be a definite mismatch. One could be an early maturer who has reached most of his or her adult height and weight while the other may be a late maturer who has not begun going through the mental and emotional upheavals of puberty. While age, height, and weight are important factors to consider, compare the relative maturity of the two players *first*, followed by all these other physical factors.

Height and Weight

Height and *weight* are important factors to consider, but do not use them without comparing all the other factors, especially those mentioned in the preceding paragraphs. Height and weight are the most common factors used for matching players in competition, so common, in fact, that we rely too much on them and give inadequate consideration to the

others. If you use height and weight in matching players for competition, remember that skill, experience, and maturity can exaggerate or nullify any height or weight advantages. It is entirely possible to have a lighter, shorter player be so much more skilled, experienced, and mature that the taller, heavier, inexperienced player would be at a disadvantage if the two faced each other in competition. You cannot consider any one of these factors discussed here by itself, but must put all of these factors together, evaluating them appropriately so that the competition is as fair as you can make it.

Age

The *age* factor in matching players needs repetition. If you are working with young players of pubescent age, be very careful about using convenient age-groupings. Having the seventh grade play games against the eighth grade is very common. Modify this if the other factors mentioned in this chapter cause you to feel that one or more of the players would be engaged in a mismatch in such a contest. Although you must consider age, do not rely on it as the sole factor in matching players. In the past, age has been used too often with little consideration given to the other factors listed above.

Mental State

In matching players, also consider the *mental state* of your participants. If it were easy to do so, we would list this factor higher in the list of priorities. But it is difficult even for professional psychologists, let alone coaches, to agree on the mental state of an individual at a given time. If you sense a player is just not ready or willing to compete against another, for whatever reason, do not force him or her to compete. Do not use embarrassment, do not use harassment, do not use any pressure to force an athlete to play.

If there is ever a time when you, the coach, must attempt to be a counselor, it is when you sense that a young player has some reservations about competing against another. Decide when it is a good time to talk to the player to determine the reason for the hesitancy or the reluctance. Then try to help in whatever way seems appropriate. If nothing else, give him or her time to work out and overcome this mental barrier to competition.

Sex

The *sex* of the players you match is the final factor you must consider. This was never a problem in the past; sex was usually the first factor considered. We had boys' teams and girls' teams and never the twain would meet. Obviously, this has changed greatly since 1972, and now boys and girls are playing sports and physical activities together more than ever before. It is against the law for any of you coaching in federally funded programs to segregate teams simply on the basis of sex. All of the other factors mentioned in the preceding paragraphs must be considered before sex, and if there is some sexual segregation, it must be based on one or more of the preceding factors, especially skill, rather than on the sex of your players. The past decade has seen a remarkable growth in participation in sport by women, especially by school-age girls. This has been primarily due to another federal law that sought to provide more equality in education, Title IX of the Educational Amendments Act of 1972.

TITLE IX OF THE EDUCATIONAL AMENDMENTS ACT OF 1972

Originally causing much consternation on the part of educators and coaches, this act has produced a remarkable increase in sports participation by young women and has brought about an astounding improvement in their sport skills. Originally, Title IX did provide a basis for sexually segregated teams and classes in such contact sports as football and wrestling, but even this has changed. Today, if you are working in a school program or a federally funded program and a young girl wants to try out for your football team, you cannot reject her just on the basis of sex. Your team may be sexually segregated, not by sex, however, but rather by skill or one of the other factors mentioned above. As one judge pointed out after seeing a roller derby, he could see no reason why women should be regarded as the weaker sex.

Some of the earlier Title IX court cases were ambivalent in their interpretation of this law, but it now clearly appears that any sexual segregation should be based on skill, not just on the sex of the participants. This is true even in collision or contact sports. Today, if you are working in a program which is affected by Title IX, the basic rule is, if a girl wants to try out for a boy's sport, you must let her. If she is rejected

from the team, it should be by an objective evaluation of her skills in that sport.

Although in recent years some court decisions which put a programmatic interpretation on Title IX (i.e., funds can only be withheld from programs that receive federal funds and few athletic programs do) have weakened Title IX, the law remains in effect, and you must follow it. Because the intent of this law was to increase the educational and athletic opportunities for young girls, it has permitted young girls to play on boys' teams, including football and wrestling. *It does not permit boys to play on girls' teams.* This may seem to be reverse discrimination, but remember, the intent of the law was to increase the educational and athletic opportunities for young women. Consequently, if a young girl wants to try out for your team, and your program and the school receives federal funds, permit her to do so, and do not exclude her from the team except on the basis of a fair objective evaluation of her skill.

RECOMMEN-DATIONS

1. Do not match players using methods which are mainly convenient.

2. First, try to match players on their skill level.

3. Next, match players as equally as possible on experience.

4. Look for injuries or incapacitating conditions which may temporarily alter the fairness of competition.

5. Age, height, weight, and maturity of the players are factors which must be considered together when matching players. Take special consideration of the relative physical, mental, and emotional maturity of your players.

6. Never force or coerce a player to perform.

7. Do not segregate your players strictly on the basis of sex.

8. Whenever applicable, follow the dictates of Title IX and allow players of both sexes to participate together, as long as all of the other factors are equal.

Your players are now ready for competition. But lurking in the background is another vital duty, an unusual one that is performed less frequently than all the others. But when it need to be performed, it becomes your most important duty. This duty is providing first aid and emergency medical care.

Chapter 8
First Aid and Emergency Medical Procedures

PROVIDING MEDICAL ASSISTANCE

When a player who is under your supervision is injured, you have the duty to provide reasonable medical assistance to the injured participant as soon as possible under the prevailing circumstances. This medical assistance does not require that you have the skills and training of a physician or an emergency medical technician, but it does require basic first aid skills and an organized system of quickly obtaining more trained medical personnel.

In the following three lawsuits coaches or agents of a sponsor of a sports activity were found guilty of negligence. Remember, in carrying out this duty, you can be negligent if you do nothing, if you select the wrong action, or if you select the correct action but perform it incorrectly.

You do have the responsibility to administer first aid and put the emergency medical system into operation, but you should not try to do too much. Unless you are well trained, it is dangerous for you to go beyond the requirements of basic first aid treatment of an injured player.

Exceeding Your Authority

The first case we will describe involved an agent of a roller skating rink in his treatment of an injury (*Clayton et al. v.*

New Dreamland Roller Skating Rink, 1951). In this New Jersey case, a woman was rollerskating at the skating rink and fell, allegedly by tripping on chewing gum left on the skating rink floor. She sustained a fracture of her left arm and was taken to the first aid room of the skating rink.

One of the officers of the skating rink corporation was summoned to administer first aid. He was asked whether or not he was a doctor and replied that he was not, but that as a prize fight manager, he had experience in such matters. He manipulated the woman's injured arm and applied traction to it despite her request that he cease any further treatment.

The court held that although the actions of the officer of the skating rink might have been performed with the best of intentions, there was a jury question as to whether his acts were appropriate under the circumstances, particularly because he did not obtain the consent of the injured woman. The court held that the jury might well have found that his actions constituted an assault and battery upon the injured woman, and the earlier dismissal of the case was in error. The appellate court ruled that the officer of the skating rink had exceeded his authority and expertise in treating the injury, and aggravated the injury.

Improper Medical Care

Improper medical care was ruled in a California case involving an injury sustained in a preseason interschool scrimmage between two high school football teams (*Welch v. Dunsmuir Joint Union High School District*, 1958). No game officials were present, but instead the coaches were on the field directing and supervising play. The injured player was a quarterback who ran the ball on a quarterback sneak and was tackled shortly after he went through the line. As he was falling forward, another player, coming in to make the tackle, fell on top of him. After the play, the quarterback was lying on his back on the field, unable to get to his feet. His coach suspected a neck injury and had the player take hold of his hands to see if there was any grip in them. The player was able to move his hands at that time.

This procedure seems appropriate so far. The player was then removed from the field by eight boys, four on each side. No backboard or firm support was used. This removal of the player from the field without the use of a stretcher was an improper medical practice in view of the symptoms. After the player had been removed from the playing field, he was unable to move his hands, fingers, and feet. A physician who testified stated it was his opinion that the player must have sustained additional damage to his spinal cord after the tackle. The player became a permanent quadriplegic because of the injury and was awarded over $200,000 in this famous 1958 decision.

**The Need
for Immediate
Medical Assistance**

Another well-known case occurred in Louisiana in the 1960s. In this instance, football players were participating in their second day of practice in the middle of August (*Mogabgab v. Orleans Parish School Board*, 1970). Shortly after 5 p.m., the players were running wind sprints. One of the players became fatigued and fell down. Two of his teammates then assisted him to the school bus. The fatigued player was nauseous and vomited prior to entering the bus and while enroute to the high school. The bus arrived at the school 20 minutes after the incident, and the injured player was placed in the shower, taken out, and laid on a blanket with another blanket over him. One of his coaches also gave him an ammonia capsule and unsuccessfully tried to give him salt water.

A first aid book was brought into the room and the coaches discussed the problem and what should be done. An hour later the parents of another player arrived at the school. They observed that the injured player was grayish-blue, his mouth hanging slightly ajar, his lips and the exposed hand and arm were bluish, and he was moaning. One of the parents told the coach that the player was critical and apparently in shock and offered to call a physician. The coach indicated that he would do so if needed. The parents then both demanded that a physician be called. The coach again stated that it was his responsibility. A physician finally was called and arrived 2 hours after the player had collapsed. He testified that he found the player

> in an obviously sick condition; that he was unconscious, cyanotic, cool, clammy, actively sweating, with no pulse in any of his major vessels, no evidence of pressure, pupils were widely dilated, fixed, and not responsive to light.

At that time he diagnosed the condition as profound heat exhaustion with shock to an advanced degree, but not necessarily irreversible. He immediately had the injured player transferred to a hospital where his condition was diagnosed as heat stroke. Early the next morning the injured player died. The jury found the coach to have been negligent because it felt that the player would have survived had he received prompt medical attention. The coaches had actively denied such attention to the player and were held negligent as agents of the school.

In each of these cases, some improper or inadequate first aid was administered. Your responsibilities in carrying out this duty include administering first aid, having access to emergency medical treatment, and completing follow-up procedures, investigations, and reports.

FIRST AID

Anyone who coaches a sport should be able to administer first aid, including cardio-pulmonary resuscitation. We would also recommend your first aid and CPR skills be reviewed and renewed periodically, so that you are able to render first aid treatment that is current and proper.

Your program should include a well-planned and organized emergency medical system. If your program does not have such a plan, or if one exists but you are uncertain about it, establish or clarify the plan so that you know exactly what to do when an emergency arises. For more information on first aid and treating sport injuries, see the *Coaches Guide to Sport Injuries* (Bergeron & Wilson, 1985), another volume in the ACEP Level 2 series of Coaches Guides.

Four Basic Duties

At the very least, coaches should be able to carry out the following four basic duties of a first aider:

1. Protect the individual from further harm and do so judiciously. Do not drag an injured player away from the practice field so that practice may continue, especially if he or she is unconscious or you suspect a head, neck, or back injury.

2. Attempt to maintain or restore life to the injured player. Artificial respiration and antichoking treatments have changed in the last decade. Are you current in your ability to render first aid?

3. Comfort and reassure the individual. Keep him or her quiet, speak to the person in reassuring tones, and keep any panic-spreaders away from the scene of the injury.

4. Immediately activate the emergency medical system.

Good Samaritan Laws

It may soothe you somewhat to know that many states have passed "good samaritan laws" which attempt to protect an individual who is rendering care at the scene of an injury, accident, or emergency. The following is an example of such a law from Montana:

> Any person licensed as a physician and surgeon under the laws of the state of Montana or any other person who in good faith renders emergency care or assistance without compensation at the scene of an emergency or accident shall not be liable for any civil damages for acts or omissions other than damages occasioned by gross negligence or by willful or wanton acts or omissions by such person in rendering such emergency care (Montana Codes Annotated, 41-1-105).

Notice the qualifications to this law: receiving compensation, gross negligence, and willful or wanton acts or omissions. Be sure to check on the status of "good samaritan laws" in your state. Does your state recognize these laws? If not, you can't depend on them for support. Better yet, be able to render adequate first aid, and have an emergency medical system.

First Aid Kit

Have available a first aid kit for your use. This kit should be stocked with all the items which may be necessary for treating injuries in your program. This kit must be accessible, clean, and neat. Its contents must be simple and easily understood. All members of your staff should be familiar with the location of the first aid kit as well as what is in it.

Be sure that after every usage, and on a regular basis, the kit is rechecked and restocked so that it and its contents remain ready for use. Some contents of a first aid kit may become chemically outdated after a long period of storage. Be sure the contents of your kit are usable. Some recommended contents for a first aid kit include the following:

- Sterile dressings, eye patches, and nonadherent dressings
- A sterile fluid, either water or saline solution to wash out lacerations
- Tape and band-aids
- Splinting material such as light wood splints or cardboard (Some authorities do *not* recommend the use of inflatable air splints because of the inherent problems with the use of these splints.)
- Elastic bandages and gauze

- Heavy-duty bandage scissors

- Flashlight with extra batteries

- Tongue blades and cotton swabs, individually wrapped and sterile

- Material for making a sling, such as a muslin sling

- Plastic bags with ice, or some of the quick-cold chemical icing agents

- Two sand bags for stabilizing suspected head and neck injuries

- Basic information, such as the Red Cross pressure points for controlling bleeding, the outline steps for CPR, and a list of emergency telephone numbers for emergency rooms, emergency transportation, and doctors' offices

EMERGENCY MEDICAL TREATMENT

The fourth duty of a first aider is to activate the emergency medical system. How this system works depends upon you, your sport, your program, and your community. The essence of this duty is that those who need further medical treatment should have access to it via a well-planned and organized program. This plan should involve your athletic trainer and school nurse if you have them available; it should include transportation of injured players; and it should enable you to contact immediately the physician and family of the injured player.

Plan to use your colleagues or assistants when deciding whether emergency transportation is necessary. You should assign someone the responsibility of summoning the emergency services if assistance is needed. Try to contact the parents of the injured player as soon as possible. You may also need to contact a physician. When you talk to the physician, be able to describe the player's condition and the first aid treatment you have rendered. Ask what you should do until the injured player can be seen or transported to the physician.

An ambulance, a designated agency, a parent, or a supervisor should transport the injured player. Your last choice should be using your personal vehicle. Great care must be taken in the transportation of any injured player to avoid aggravating the injury.

In summary, *it is essential your emergency medical treatment plan provides immediate access to trained medical personnel.* It is especially important this emergency system emphasizes communication between you and the trained medical personnel available to you.

FOLLOW-UP PROCEDURES AND REPORTS

Accident Reports

Following an injury, you should investigate the cause of the injury as thoroughly as possible to see what factors, if any, contributed to the injury and which of these factors can be corrected or eliminated. Try to find the cause of the injury and keep any evidence of that cause. If the injury was due to a remediable condition, try to eliminate the condition, or if you cannot, report the nature of the condition to your supervisor.

If the injury is of a serious nature, write up a report of the injury. A copy of the accident report form recommended by the National Safety Council is shown on page 76. It could easily be adapted for use in your program. When you write this report, keep it simple but thorough: Be complete, precise, accurate, orderly, and, most important, *objective* in your description. Do not try to be diagnostic; do not engage in prognosis; and do not be defensive. Then in the lower right hand corner, note any recommendations you have for preventing similar accidents. It is very important you consider this and to try to reduce the likelihood of another similar injury as best you can.

STANDARD STUDENT ACCIDENT REPORT FORM

Part A. Information on *All* Accidents

1. Name _____ Home address _____

2. School _____ Sex M ☐ F ☐ Age _____ Grade _____

3. Time accident occurred: Hour _____ AM _____ PM   Date: _____

4. Place of accident: School building ☐, school grounds ☐, to or from school ☐, home ☐, elsewhere ☐

5. Nature of injury:

			Description of Accident:
Abrasion ☐	Concussion ☐	Puncture ☐	
Amputation ☐	Cut ☐	Scalds ☐	
Asphyxiation ☐	Dislocation ☐	Scratches ☐	
Bite ☐	Fracture ☐	Shock (elec.) ☐	
Bruise ☐	Laceration ☐	Sprain ☐	
Burn ☐	Poisoning ☐	Other (specify) ☐	

Part of body injured:

Abdomen ☐	Eye ☐	Other ☐	
Ankle ☐	Face ☐	Leg ☐	
Arm ☐	Finger ☐	Mouth ☐	
Back ☐	Foot ☐	Nose ☐	
Chest ☐	Hand ☐	Scalp ☐	
Ear ☐	Head ☐	Tooth ☐	
Elbow ☐	Knee ☐	Wrist ☐	

6. Degree of injury: Death ☐, permanent impairment ☐, temporary disability ☐, nondisabling ☐

7. Total number of days lost from school _____ (to be filled in on return)

Part B. Additional Information on School Jurisdiction Accident:

8. Teacher in charge when accident occurred (name) _____
   Present at scene of accident: No ☐ Yes ☐

9. Immediate action taken:
   First aid treatment ☐ By (name) _____

   Sent to school nurse ☐ By (name) _____

   Sent home ☐ By (name) _____

   Sent to physician ☐ By (name) _____

       Physician's name _____

   Sent to hospital ☐ By (name) _____

       Hospital name _____

10. Was a parent or other individual notified? No ☐ Yes ☐ When _____

    How _____ Name of individual notified _____

    By whom? (enter name) _____

11. Witnesses: 1. Name _____ Address _____
    2. Name _____ Address _____

12. Location:

			Remarks:
Athletic field _____	Locker _____		
Auditorium _____	Pool _____		
Cafeteria _____	Sch. grounds _____		
Classroom _____	_____ shop _____		
Corridor _____	Showers _____		
Dressing room _____	Stairs _____		
Gymnasium _____	Toilets and _____		
Home Econ. _____	washrooms		
Laboratories _____	Other _____		
	(specify)		

Signed: (Principal) _____ (Teacher) _____

National Safety Council: reprinted with permission.

Record Keeping

In the event of a serious injury, keep copies of your injury report, and be sure they are written so you will be able to remember exactly what took place. This is especially important if you are coaching young athletes. Because they are minors, their right to bring suit is held for them from 1 to 3 years after they reach legal age. *It is possible you may be called to account for an injury that occurred 8 or 9 years ago*, so your injury report should be thorough and accurate enough that you can recall the incident and the related conditions with clarity.

Confidential Information

One additional point about injuries needs mention: Disclosure of medical information without consent is a potential source of liability. If a college coach is interested in one of your players and asks about previous injuries, you should give no information other than the nature of the injury and the method of treatment (e.g., "It was a leg injury which required no operation"). Anything else will probably go beyond your expertise and may be a violation of privileged, confidential information. To avoid situations in which your unwillingness to discuss an athlete's medical history might restrict the player's chances of receiving a scholarship offer, you can refer all questions concerning injuries to the athlete's physician and to the athlete.

RECOMMEN-DATIONS

1. You are responsible for carrying out the four basic duties of the first aider:

  - Protect the individual from further harm.
  - Attempt to maintain or restore life.
  - Comfort and reassure the injured player.
  - Activate the emergency medical system.

2. Be sure you are confident in your first aid knowledge and techniques.

3. Be aware of the status of "good samaritan laws" in your state.

4. Have a well-stocked first aid kit available. Be sure you know where it is, its contents, and how to use those contents.

5. Develop a plan for providing emergency medical care. This program must emphasize communication so that your injured players can rapidly receive the care they need.

6. Be very careful when moving or transporting injured players. Use your own vehicle only as a last resort.

7. Develop your emergency care plan in consultation with physicians, athletic trainers, nurses, administrators,

parents, and other interested parties who may be available to you.

8. Following an injury, investigate the cause of the injury and take steps to remedy any conditions which may have caused or enhanced the injury.

9. Write and keep an objective descriptive report of all serious injuries. Remember, if the players you coach are minors, keep this record for several years after the injury.

10. Do not disclose medical information other than the nature of the injury and the type of treatment rendered without the consent of the player and his parents.

11. For more information on first aid or treating sports injuries consult the *Coaches Guide to Sport Injuries* (Bergeron & Wilson, 1985).

You have now learned the seven most important legal duties of a coach. Some other concerns you should consider when you coach are discussed in the final two chapters.

Chapter 9
Player, Official, and Spectator Rights

SPECIFIC LEGAL CONCERNS

You need to be aware of some other legal concerns in addition to the specific legal duties we have already discussed. In this chapter we will examine specific concerns relevant to your role as a coach; chapter 10 will present general concerns.

Most of the specific legal concerns are the result of recent court decisions which have added some new responsibilities to your job as a coach. One specific concern is for the safety of spectators and bystanders. This is not new, but many coaches may not be familiar with their legal position. First, however, we will review some considerations you should make in regard to player rights, player-versus-player lawsuits, and the responsibilities of game officials.

PLAYER RIGHTS

Autocracy Versus Democracy

Not too long ago being autocratic or dictatorial as a coach was widely accepted. However, this has changed in the past two decades because the legal rights of athletes are increasingly recognized. Even the formally sacrosanct rules and regulations of athletic governing agencies now state that high school athletic associations and sport associations such as the Little League must recognize the rights of their participants.

The emphasis on player rights also requires a change in teaching and coaching methodology. Coaches are being asked to change their styles and methods of interacting with players so that a more open atmosphere prevails. Players today have more questions and are more willing to ask those questions. Coaches generally need to be more willing to listen to these questions and comments of their players. We would encourage you to adopt the cooperative coaching style discussed in

Coaching Young Athletes (Martens, Christina, Harvey, & Sharkey, 1980), the ACEP Level 1 text, and become more of a guide and a leader than a dictator.

Players on your teams, whether in a school program or not, have the same rights of any other citizen with the exception of those rights that are reserved for those of legal age. Courts have especially emphasized that your athletes are not subject to arbitrary or capricious rules or procedures. Most of the emphasis on player rights have involved freedom of expression, freedom of religion, freedom from discrimination, the right of due process, and the right of confidentiality.

Free Expression

Be very careful about placing any restrictions on your players which stifles their right of free expression. A restriction is permissible only if it eliminates a danger in your sport. This includes hair and dress codes, and symbolic expression. In most states, it is difficult for you to control your players dress or the way they wear their hair unless safety is a factor. If your players decide they want to wear an armband in support of the antinuclear crusade, you should allow them to do so. This is particularly true if your team is part of a school-sponsored sport program.

In the past, coaches were able to set and enforce dress, hair, and conduct codes. On many campuses in the late 1960s and early 1970s, a clear distinction existed between the jock image and the visible counter-culture image. In one campus incident, the crew-cut members of the ROTC department, with crew-cut athletes and coaches standing next to them, blocked an antiwar demonstration.

Today, this distinction has virtually disappeared, and perhaps the topic of freedom of expression is not applicable to you. But you should be aware that recent court decisions have consistently supported students' and athletes' rights to exercise their freedom of expression, including symbolic expression. For these reasons, when you establish codes of conduct for your teams, or when you discuss the expected social behavior of your athletes, you must allow the players to express their concerns and desires about the rules and standards. This has an added advantage in that rules and regulations developed and endorsed by the group are more likely to be adhered to by all group members.

Religious Rights

Avoid infringing on the religious rights of your athletes. If one of your players has valid religious reasons for not participating on a day that is special to him or her, do not get angry and do not try to force the player to participate. The right to freely exercise one's religion is an important right in our society and should not be influenced by the dictates of a coach or teacher.

In a recent Michigan case, the physical education class included members of a religion who were concerned about the immodest attire worn during physical education class (*Moody v. Cronin*, 1979). Although they might see the same parts of the body in other classes, they were not surrounded by bare arms and legs as they were in physical education classes. Furthermore, because all students wore gym uniforms, it was impossible for them to follow the dictates of their religion which included denying themselves a second look at certain parts of the anatomy. While this denial was possible in other classes, it was not in physical education classes because of the uniforms. The court ruled that the students had the right to follow the tenets of their religion, and the school was ordered to come up with another method for teaching physical education to these students.

Rights of Due Process

It is essential you allow your players the right of due process. This is the right to be treated fairly and not be denied liberty, property, or the pursuit of happiness without being given the chance to defend oneself.

To assure fairness, follow, at the very least, a three-step procedure. First, explain to your players any rules you are enforcing so they understand them. Second, if the rules are violated, the player must be informed of what was done wrong. Third, and most important, the player must then be given the chance to defend him or herself. In cases of more

severe penalties, such as suspension or dismissal from a team, due process may involve more, including perhaps a formal hearing. But in all cases, use this three-step procedure before making any judgments.

Avoid Discrimination

Participants in athletic programs, especially those in schools or other federally-funded organizations, should be free from discrimination. Some discrimination, particularly age limits for participation, is allowed (although even these have been successfully challenged in a few instances). But, for the most part, any discrimination on your part is forbidden. As we have already mentioned in various parts of this guide, discrimination should not be made on the basis of sex or physical or mental handicaps. We might now add that discrimination on the basis of race or ethnic origin is similarly forbidden.

Confidentiality

Remember, your participants have the right to confidentiality in certain matters. We have already discussed the danger of giving out medical information without player approval. The same applies to grades if you are teaching or coaching in a program in which participants receive grades.

An interesting incident illustrated this right to confidentiality in a California school whose physical education program stressed physical fitness. To motivate the students to higher levels of fitness, the students were given uniforms indicating their fitness status. Some parents challenged this practice because it violated the students' rights to receive a confidential grade. Wearing the uniform in essence indicated the grade the students were to receive. The school was able to defend itself in this situation, proving that the physical fitness scores were only one of several factors in determining students' grades; the uniforms reflected only their physical fitness status, and not necessarily the grades the students would receive. Therefore, the school was allowed to continue the practice.

PLAYER VERSUS PLAYER LAWSUITS

In the past 14 years, a trend has been for players either to be the object of a lawsuit, or more recently, to sue other players for playing negligently. Some of the first lawsuits of this nature involved criminal charges against hockey players for assault and battery on the ice.

The newer suits are interesting because they contain allegations of negligence by one player toward another on the playing field. These lawsuits have shown that players do have a duty to other players, and if there is a breach of that duty which is a substantial factor in a resulting injury, the player can be found negligent. Lawsuits of this nature have occurred, and are occurring, in football, basketball, soccer, and softball. The circumstances surrounding some of these negligence suits are described next.

Intentional Injury

In a lawsuit involving football players, a defensive back was blindsided by a fullback during the course of play (*Hackbart v. Cincinnati Bengals*, 1977). The act was blatant and in violation of National Football League rules. Kneeling on the ground, the defensive back was watching a pass play being completed from the other side of the field as the other player came up behind him and struck him in the back of the helmet. This case went all the way to the United States Supreme Court which held that the intentional infliction of an injury by one player upon another can give rise to tort liability and permitted the defensive back to sue the other player and his team.

A similar and highly publicized incident occurred in professional basketball. A player ran toward midcourt where a skirmish was under way (Woolf, 1980). As he arrived, a player from the opposing team turned and struck the on-rushing player in the face. The injured player suffered a fractured

skull, fractured jaw, broken nose, and other facial injuries. He was disabled for the remainder of the season and asked for $2,650,000 in damages. The jury found that the striking player acted with "reckless disregard for the safety" of others and awarded the injured player $3,300,000. It is significant to note that the owners of the striking player's team were held responsible for the unacceptable behavior of the guilty player and ordered to pay the judgment. Clearly, this decision has far-reaching implications for school boards, sports administrators, and game officials.

Violating Safety Rules

In Illinois, two teams of high school age boys were playing a soccer match (*Nabozny v. Barnhill*, 1975). One of the players kicked the ball toward the goal, and two players chased after it. The goalie's teammate reached the ball first and kicked the ball to the goalie. The opposing player kept chasing the ball. The goalie went down on his left knee, received the pass, pulled the ball to his chest, and held the ball with both hands. The opposing player kicked at the ball, in violation of the rules of soccer, and struck the goalie in the left side of the head causing severe injuries. All the witnesses agreed that the opposing player had time to avoid contact with the goalie, and that the goalie had remained in the penalty area in front of the goal.

The court held that when a safety rule is contained in a recognized set of rules governing the conduct of athletic competition, a participant in such competition, trained and coached by knowledgeable personnel, is charged with a legal duty to every other participant to refrain from conduct proscribed by the safety rule. Hence, the jury found the opposing player's conduct negligent.

Softball has also seen at least two player-versus-player lawsuits with similar circumstances. In a Louisiana case, a member of one team ran 4 to 5 feet out of the baseline in an attempt to break up a double play at second base (*Bourque v. Duplechin*, 1976). He collided with the second baseman, and as he did so, he brought his left arm up under the second baseman's chin. The injured player, 70 pounds lighter than the baserunner, suffered a fractured jaw and had eight teeth knocked out or broken. The court held that the baserunner was under the duty to play softball in an ordinary fashion without unsportsmanlike conduct, and that he breached this duty by his actions. He was found negligent.

A similar incident occurred just recently in North Dakota. A catcher in a softball league game has contended he was permanently crippled with knee injuries after a player on the opposing team threw a shoulder block into him as he tried to score. The injured player has asked for $203,400 in damages with litigation still in process.

Athletes'
Legal Duties

What does all this mean to you? Player-versus-player negligence suits are a new trend in sports injury litigation. At the very least, these lawsuits mean you should inform your players not only to play fairly and within the rules, but that they have a legal duty to do so. You should inform your players that if they do not play within the rules and in a sportsmanlike manner, they might be charged with negligence. Some authorities feel that these types of lawsuits are likely to increase. Be sure your players realize they can be negligent in the way they play the game. They do owe a duty to other players.

GAME OFFICIALS

Securing good game officials for your contests to help you assure the game is played safely and within the rules is also becoming more important. However, this poses a problem: Probably no two coaches agree on just exactly what a good official is.

Try to obtain trained and experienced officials, because if you hire these officials, they may be regarded as your agent. In other words, if an official you have hired is sued, you could well be listed as co-defendant. Certainly you can do more than one campus recreation intramural agency did in advertising for basketball officials. Because of a persistent problem in obtaining game officials, good or otherwise, every year the agency would send the following flyer around campus.

> THIS WINTER ENJOY A REWARDING CAREER AS A CAMPUS RECREATION INTRAMURAL BASKETBALL REFEREE. QUALIFICATIONS: APPLICANTS MUST BE ABLE TO:
>
> 1. RUN FORWARD AND/OR BACKWARD.
>
> 2. BLOW A WHISTLE.
>
> 3. MAKE SPLIT SECOND DECISIONS AFFECTING THE LIVES OF TEN OR MORE PEOPLE.
>
> 4. HAVE A VAGUE UNDERSTANDING OF THE GAME OF BASKETBALL.

Defending yourself for an injury caused by poor officiating based on this listing of qualifications would be quite difficult. While this advertisement was written tongue-in-cheek, and a training program was provided for officials, it would have been better to be more serious and precise in listing required qualifications. According to the *National Law Journal*, in the decade ahead our courts will assuredly be called upon to determine whether a sports official can be held liable for an injury sustained by a player during an athletic contest (Narol & Dedopoulos, 1972). Some already have been. If you are an

official, or if you choose to train or hire officials, be aware that this duty is one the courts will quite likely further examine in the near future. We expect this to be a trend in sports injury litigation.

SPECTATORS AND BYSTANDERS

Common Knowledge Rules

In most cases, spectators assume the reasonable risks of watching a contest. The next time you go to see a major league baseball game, read the back of the ticket you purchase. You may be surprised to find you have agreed to a valid waiver or release of liability printed on the back of the ticket. These exculpatory clauses have been upheld because courts have applied a "common knowledge" rule to spectators at sports events. The rule states the risks posed to spectators are so widely known that people of reasonable intelligence could not help but realize their potentiality, and must, for that reason, be deemed to have accepted or assumed the risk of injury.

Exceptions

You need to be aware of some exceptions to this "common knowledge" rule. First, the operator of an area must meet a standard of care in providing facilities for spectators. If you have bleachers on your field and they collapse under the weight of the crowd, this could certainly be considered negligence and a risk that is unreasonable and is not of common knowledge. Fortunately, it is also not a common occurrence.

Second, if you provide a protected area for spectators, you must provide adequate protection. One of the risks you assume as you watch a baseball game is the risk of being struck by a batted or thrown ball. If you have a seat behind a protective screen, the screen must be in good enough condition to prevent batted or thrown balls from coming through it.

A third exception occurs with sports new to a locale. If the sport is very new, it might be assumed that the spectators had no basis for having the common knowledge necessary to watch the sport safely. Therefore, if your sport is new in your area, you may need to educate or warn the spectators of possible risks and do what you can to minimize these risks until they do become a matter of common knowledge.

Fourth, spectators do not assume the risk of unreasonable conduct by the players. If one of your basketball players in frustration violently kicks the ball into the stands injuring a spectator, the common knowledge rule might not apply. Nor should players assume the risk of unreasonable conduct by the spectators. Negligence was found in one instance where spectators were allowed to crowd onto a field, creating a hazard for the players.

Bystanders

Generally, you have no duty to bystanders, but exceptional conditions may give you such a duty. If your baseball field is immediately adjacent to a busy roadway, you should take some precautions to protect passing motorists from the play of the game and your players from the passing motorists. An interesting lawsuit illustrates how a bystander may recover damages from the unreasonable actions of a player (*Bonetti v. Double Play Tavern*, 1954).

During a league championship baseball game in California in the bottom of the ninth with the score tied, the left fielder

dropped a fly ball and the winning run was scored. In disgust and anger, the left fielder picked up the dropped ball and threw it out of the field across an adjacent street in the direction of a service station. A woman who was walking to her car was struck by the ball on the side of the head and knocked to the ground. The court held that the player's action was negligent. Furthermore, because the uniforms were provided by a local tavern, the player was an agent of that tavern. Consequently, the sponsor of the team was responsible for the negligence of the player, and the woman was able to collect $3000 in damages. This is an exceptional case; usually you owe little, if any, duty to bystanders and passers-by, but it is possible.

RECOMMEN-DATIONS

1. Be open in your communication with your players. Be a cooperative style rather than a command style coach.

2. Respect your players' right to freedom of expression, including symbolic expression.

3. Do not be arbitrary or capricious in setting rules or standards of conduct for your players. Develop these rules and standards with your players.

4. Never intrude on the religious beliefs of your players.

5. Be sure your players know what is expected of them. If they violate a rule, be sure you tell them precisely what it was they did wrong and give them a chance to explain their side of the story.

6. Do not discriminate against your players, especially on the basis of race, sex, or handicapping conditions.

7. Do not violate your players' right to confidentiality in certain matters. Some of what you do must be regarded as a privileged communication, not to be passed on to third parties.

8. Warn your players about player-versus-player lawsuits. Explain to them that if they play with blatant disregard for the rules or in an unsportsmanlike manner, they may be charged with negligence.

9. Select, train, or obtain good officials for your contests. Remember, these officials may be regarded as agents of either you or your sponsoring organization.

10. If you are an official, you must be a reasonable and a prudent official.

11. Remember the "common knowledge" rule as it applies to spectators and the exceptions to this rule.

12. Protect, as best you can, spectators and bystanders from the actions of your players and the risks of the game, and vice-versa.

Chapter 10
Record Keeping, Transportation, and Insurance

ADDITIONAL GENERAL CONCERNS

In this chapter three issues which indirectly affect your coaching are discussed, and recommendations are made about each topic to help you protect yourself in the event of litigation. These topics have not been the focus of many lawsuits in sport, but an awareness of some salient points about each topic will help you to better perform your legal duties.

RECORDS AND RECORD KEEPING

We have mentioned records and record keeping several times in this guide. The topic, however, is worthy of consideration on its own because it reflects on how you have carried out your other duties. The following is sound advice.

1. Organize a complete record-keeping system. These records should contain all of your written plans for instruction, the plan for emergency medical care and other emergencies, the health history of your participants, the participation history of your players, a form indicating the risks of the activity signed and dated by your participants and, if necessary, by their parents, and, of course, all accident and injury reports. Because you must retain these records for some time, organization of a storage and retrieval system is essential.

2. The format of the written record should be simple but complete. Emphasize clarity when designing these forms and especially when filling out your reports. This need for clarity is particularly important for your injury or accident reports.

3. Take care in filling out your reports. Be thorough, but try to be descriptive and objective. Try to adopt a neutral style of writing when completing reports, especially injury and accident reports. Do not go beyond your abilities and do not try to diagnose an injury. Be sure to describe the first aid rendered and the time you contacted medical personnel if it was necessary. Remember, when coaching minors, a lawsuit may be filed years after the injury.

4. Participate in and stay current with any athletic injury reporting systems which may be in operation in your sport. If you are aware of and participate in these systems, you will be better aware of injuries in your sport and defects in technique or equipment that need to be remedied. You also will be better able to explain to your players the risks they face when participating in your sport.

TRANSPOR-TATION

Athletes are transported to games everyday. In the majority of cases, this is done safely, but there have been some notable exceptions. In the early 1970s, two college football teams were devastated by plane crashes. Just a few years ago, a college basketball team suffered the same fate. Some professional athletes have retired early in their careers because of fears associated with the travel necessary in sport.

The risks associated with travel are quite varied. Some of you face the problem of fighting busy freeway travel, while we in Montana are sometimes faced with traveling 600 miles one way under adverse weather conditions for a football play-off game. Whatever your situation, if travel is involved, plan prudently to provide the best means of travel you can. In doing this, you should be aware of a number of factors which have arisen in regard to transporting players to games.

Choosing Transportation

Your best choice, if it is available and you can afford it, is to use a licensed commercial carrier and to sign an agreement with this carrier placing the responsibility for safe transportation on the carrier. Public carriers, especially those involved in interstate transportation, are usually required to maintain their vehicles to higher specifications than school districts, recreational and sport programs, and individuals. In addition, laws require common carriers to maintain adequate liability insurance for the benefit of their passengers. Using a common carrier is your best choice, but, unfortunately, it is expensive

and may put you at the mercy of their schedule rather than yours.

A good alternative is to use the vehicle of the agency for whom you work. If you coach in a school-sponsored program, use the school vehicles. If you find you must drive one of the school vehicles yourself, be sure to understand local and state law regarding those who drive such vehicles. It is possible this may require you to have additional qualifications as a driver. In some states, no person may drive any school bus transporting school children or any motor vehicle for the transportation of persons for compensation until he has been licensed as a chauffeur.

We do not recommend you use your own personal vehicle for transporting players. This is your worst choice. But if you do, be sure you are properly licensed, your vehicle is in good condition, and your insurance applies. In some states, your vehicle may be considered a temporary substitute vehicle and may be covered by your school district's insurance policy.

Be sure that the use of your vehicle does not void your insurance policy, particularly if you are receiving any form of compensation for the use of your vehicle. If you cannot afford a common carrier, and if vehicles such as school buses are not available, it is probably better for you to let the parents transport players to the practices and games, or for the players to be responsible for their own transportation.

Transportation Responsibility in School Sport Programs

This last recommendation does not apply to school-sponsored sport programs where the school retains the responsibility for transporting students to and from competitive events. The following example illustrates the dangers of allowing students to transport themselves:

In a California school, it had been the practice for the tennis coach to arrange for team members who had cars to take their teammates without cars home (*Hanson et al. v. Reedley Joint Union High School District*, 1941). This was necessary because practice ended after the last school buses had departed. The players who used their cars were given a gallon of gasoline from the school gas pump for each 10 miles traveled. One of the cars used for this transportation had been somewhat modified. Equipped with a special carburetor and a high compression head in order to give it more speed and power, it had no fenders, no running board, no top and no horn. Plus, it had faulty lights, the speedometer was about 12 miles too slow, the tires were worn and smooth, and the steering wheel was so loose it was necessary to spin it a quarter of the way around before it took effect. Furthermore, the seat had been so lowered that the heads of the occupants came just above the doors, and when three people were in the front seat, their knees stuck up making it practically impossible for the driver to reach the emergency brake. The brakes were faulty to the extent that when the car was traveling at high speeds, they were totally inadequate.

On the way home from tennis practice, the car was involved in an accident, one student was killed and another seriously injured. The court held that the school district was liable for any negligence on the part of its employee in handling the school activity. Regardless of whether the coach was authorized to provide transportation or not, he undertook to do so, so it was his duty to exercise the same care as a reasonably prudent coach would have used under the circumstances. The court held that the coach had the opportunity to see the car and to know it was defective. Because he also knew of the driver's tendency to be reckless, he was negligent in permitting this vehicle to be used.

Negligence in Selecting and Supervising Transportation

Transportation does not have to involve a vehicle. It is not uncommon for participants to meet at a central facility and walk to a practice area. In a recent Louisiana case, some coaches for a Special Olympics basketball team were negligent because of the manner in which they supervised their charges as they walked to a gymnasium three blocks from their own developmental center (*Foster v. Houston General Insurance Company*, 1982). The first time the coaches used this route, five or six of the students broke from the group and started running away. Because one of the coaches had remained behind, the other coach had two groups of special olympic athletes at different corners of a busy intersection where the traffic was backed up. One of the players ran out into the street, was struck by a vehicle, suffered a serious injury, and later died. The court held that both coaches were negligent in the manner they chose to transport their players this three-block distance and in the manner they carried out their supervision of this transportation.

INSURANCE

Transportation Insurance

We have checked with three different insurance companies, all well known, using standardized automobile policies. In every instance, compensation for the use of a personal vehicle *voided* the personal liability section of the insurance. Remember, also, that compensation does not necessarily mean monetary remuneration. In some states, any benefit received that is motivating in nature is regarded as compensation. It is far better to place the responsibility for safe transportation of your players on some agency or group other than yourself. If you do use your vehicle, you may need to have a chauffeur's license, and you may have to purchase additional insurance. This additional liability insurance is often quite expensive.

In summary, choose your method of transportation prudently. If you decide to use your personal vehicle, be aware that this may void the personal liability section of your insurance.

Personal Liability

Because of the increase in sports injury litigation, and because of the increasing amounts of money awarded in these lawsuits, it is essential for anyone who coaches a sport to have personal liability coverage. At the minimum, you should carry $500,000 worth of personal liability insurance, and if the risks of injury are high in your sport,we recommend you double that amount.

How do you obtain this coverage at minimal cost? First, if you are a coach in a school, check to see if the school carrier has personal liability insurance. Be sure to check whether this insurance covers you for all of your duties. These policies will probably cover you while coaching the tennis team but may not cover you while you are giving private lessons to nonschool players. Indeed, if you are self-employed in the sense of giving private sport lessons, it is probable that liability insurance will be quite expensive while you give these private lessons.

Business Pursuits Coverage

If your agency does not have personal liability insurance for you, you could possibly obtain "business pursuits" insurance coverage through your homeowner's or renter's insurance, or through a variety of professional organizations. However, this "business pursuits" policy does not cover liability arising from self-employment, that is, conducting dance, gymnasium, and other classes where participants are charged a fee. It only covers you for the performance of your duties in connection with gainful employment as a coach or instructor.

If you coach a Little League baseball team or give private lessons in a sport, check with your sponsoring agency to see if you have insurance. If you do not, contact a reputable insurance agent to see what types of insurance are available to you. Be sure that your insurance covers you for the activity you are coaching and make sure you understand the specific provisions and limitations of your personal liability insurance coverage.

Health and Accident Insurance

Insuring players in your sports program through a comprehensive health and accident insurance policy is also a good idea. You and your coaches should be aware of this insurance coverage so that when accidents do happen, you can inform your players of the proper procedures to follow in filing claims. Unfortunately, many of these comprehensive health and accident insurances are inadequate, so find the best coverage you can for your athletes.

Currently, a promising new type of insurance policy is being used on a very limited basis. This is a policy designed for athletic programs, and is sometimes referred to as a "catastrophic lifetime medical liability plan." One such plan costs one dollar per participant and only covers accidents or injuries resulting from extra-curricular or co-curricular activities such as school athletics. As compared to older catastrophic insurance policies with a $50,000-$60,000 limit, this policy covers the participants for damages up to $5,000,000 including medical rehabilitation and work loss payments and even other rehabilitation costs, such as the remodeling of houses or vehicles for injured players.

Although very new, this type of policy may become increasingly available in the future. This particular policy defines a catastrophic injury as any in which the total cost of care or damage exceeds $10,000. As such, it is not intended to provide basic insurance coverage, but only coverage beyond the normal limits of insurance plans. If this type of coverage is available to you, purchase it for your players, especially in collision and contact sports.

RECOMMEN-DATIONS

1. Keep clear and thorough records of your coaching plans, medical and participation history of your participants, and accident and injury reports.

2. Be descriptive and objective when filling out accident or injury reports.

3. Stay current with athletic injury reporting systems in your sport.

4. When possible, use commercial carriers for transporting players for practice or competition. If not, use an agency vehicle. If neither of these are available, have the parents or players provide their own transportation. Use your own personal vehicle as a last resort, and be sure that such use does not void your insurance coverage. Be sure you are properly licensed to transport players if you do so.

5. If your players must walk from one area to another through traffic, select the safest route possible and closely supervise this movement.

6. Cover yourself with adequate personal liability insurance when you coach. At this time we recommend at least $500,000 of liability insurance.

7. Be sure your liability insurance covers you for all instances when you or coaching. Be aware of the limitations of your personal liability coverage.

8. Provide a comprehensive health and accident insurance policy for your participants, or have the parents or players provide this insurance for themselves.

9. Check to see if any catastrophic lifetime medical liability plans are available for your athletes, and if so, try to get this insurance coverage for your players.

Conclusion

Obviously, today's coach needs to be aware of the legal duties facing all coaches. As the volume of sport litigation increases and the money awarded in these lawsuits multiplies, it is critical you understand and seriously consider implementing the recommendations made in this *Coaches Guide to Sport Law*.

Although some of the recommendations may seem to be insignificant, minor details frequently become major considerations in sports-related lawsuits. We urge you to give a great deal of thought to the manner in which you perform your legal duties as a coach. At the present time, there is a slightly better than one-in-ten chance a coach will be involved in a sports-related lawsuit during his or her career. The cases we have described here, along with literally hundreds of other cases we have reviewed, convince us that the coaches involved in sport injury litigation are those who have failed to carry out one or more of the legal duties we have described.

It is not our intent to frighten you away from the satisfying, rewarding, and challenging experience of coaching a sport; however, it is our intent to describe to you the challenge that your legal duties present. Your legal duties, and the manner in which you fulfill these duties, are more important than ever in American sport. So don't let these legal duties deter you, but instead let them aid you in safely coaching your sport.

Use this guide and the other guides in the ACEP Level 2 series to change your coaching techniques and to avoid the practices which have produced sport injury litigation. Now that you have finished reading this guide, you are advised to work through the questions and exercises in the *Sport Law Study Guide* (Jefferies, 1985). The recommendations we have given will help you to balance fun and learning with safety. Our judicial system has made and continues making recommendations to coaches, and it is up to you to apply these in practice.

We cannot guarantee that adherence to these recommendations will eliminate a negligence suit. The law is dynamic and precludes such guarantees. We do feel, however, that our recommendations will make you better able to meet the demands the courts are placing on those who coach a sport. Your task is to balance fun with safety, competition with fair play, and speedy improvement in sport skills with sound coaching practices, and to be as reasonable and as prudent as you possibly can in carrying out these tasks.

References

Allen, R.B. (1978). Lawyers, law, and baseball. *American Bar Association Journal*, **64**, 1530-1535.

American Medical Association. (1977, September). *Medical evaluation of the athlete—A Guide*. Chicago: American Medical Association.

Appenzeller, H. (1978). *Athletics and the law*. Charlottesville, VA: The Michie Company.

Ardoin et al. v. Evangeline Parish School Board, 376 S. 2d 372 (La. App. 1979).

Arnold, D.E. (1983). *Legal considerations in the administration of public school physical education and athletic programs*. Springfield, IL: Charles C. Thomas.

Arnold, D.E. (1978, November-December). Sports product liability. *Joper*, **49**, 25-28.

Assistance for Education of All Handicapped Children Act. 20 U.S.C.S. Par. 1411 et. seq.—P.L. 94-142.

Athletics. (1973). *Law and contemporary problems*, **38**(1).

Bellman v. San Francisco High School District, 11 Cal. 2d 576, 81 P. 2d 894 (1938).

Bergeron, J.D., & Wilson, H. (1985). *Coaches guide to sport injuries*. Champaign, IL: Human Kinetics.

Bonetti v. Double Play Tavern, 274 P. 2d 751 (1954).

Bourque v. Duplechin, 331 S. 2d 40 (La. App. 1976).

Brahatcek v. Millard School District No. 17, 273 N.W. 2d 680 (Nebraska 1979).

Carpenter, L.J., & Acosta, R.V. (1980, September). Violence in sport—Is it part of the game or the intentional tort of battery? *Joper*, **51**, 18.

Carrafiello, V.A. (1980). Jocks are people too: The constitution comes to the locker room. *Creighton Law Review*, **13**, 843-862.

Child Abuse Prevention and Treatment Act. 42 U.S.C.S. Par. 5101 et. seq.—P.L. 93-247.

Cirillo v. City of Milwaukee, 34 Wis. 2d 705, 150 N.W. 2d 460 (1967).

Clayton et al. v. New Dreamland Roller Skating Rink, 14 N.J. Super. 390 (1951).

Clarke, K. (1980, May). The health supervision loop in sport. *The Physician and Sports Medicine*, **8**, 109-113.

Dailey v. Los Angeles Unified School District, 84 Cal. Rptr. 325, Vac. 87 Cal Rptr. 376, 470 P. 2d 360 (1970).

Davis, V.J. (1981). Sports liability: Blowing the whistle on the referee. *Pacific Law Journal,* **12**, 937-964.

Degooyer v. Harkness, 70 S.D. 26, 13 N.W. 2d 815 (1944).

Drowatzky, J.N. (1977). On the firing line: Negligence in physical education. *Journal of Law and Education,* **6**, 481-490.

Ecker, T. (1977, May). Will we allow the courts to kill sports? *Athletic Journal,* **57**, 12-13.

Foster v. Houston General Insurance Company, 407 S. 2d 759 (La. App. 1982).

Frazier, C.S. (1979, May-June). Sports litigation! The new attitude. *Coach and Athlete,* **41**, 11.

Frazier, C.S. (1978, April). Coaches legally accountable to athletes. *Coach and Athlete,* **40**, 14.

Graham, L.S. (1982, June). New look in sports, new faces in our courts. *Joperd,* **53**, 34.

Grant v. Lake Oswego School District #7, Clackamas County, 515 P. 2d 947 (Or. App. 1974).

Gregory, I.F. II, & Goldsmith, A. (1980, March). The sports spectator as plaintiff. *Trial,* **16**, 26-29.

Grieve, A. (1969). *The legal aspects of athletics.* New York: A.S. Barnes and Co.

Hackbart v. Cincinnati Bengals, 435 F. Supp. 352 (D. Ct. of Col. 1977). 601 F. 2d 516 (U.S. Court of Appeals, 1979).

Hanson et al. v. Reedley Joint Union High School District, 43 Cal. 2d 643, 111 P. 2d 415 (1941).

Harris, R. (1977). *The trampoline for physical education.* San Mateo, CA: The Pea Press.

Herbert, W.G., & Herbert, D.L. (1975, June). Legal aspects of physical fitness testing. *Joperd,* **46**, 17-19.

Hewitt v. Miller, 521 P. 2d 244 (Wash. App. 1974).

Hurt, W.T. (1976, April). Elements of tort liability as applied to athletic injuries. *Journal of School Health,* **46**, 200-203.

Hutter, D.M. (1975, October). Legal liability in physical education and athletics. *Physical Educator,* **35**, 160-163.

Injuries resulting from nonintentional acts in organized contact sports: The theories of recovery available to the injured athlete. *Indiana Law Review,* **12**, 687.

Jefferies, S.C. (1985). *Sport law study guide.* Champaign, IL: Human Kinetics.

Keesee v. Board of Education of the City of New York, 235 N.Y.S. 2d 300 (1962).

Landers v. School District No. 203, O'Fallon, 383 N.E. 2d 645 (Illinois 1978).

Langerman, S., & Fidel, N. (1977, January). Responsibility is also part of the game. *Trial,* **13**(1), p. 23.

Martens, R., Christina, R.W., Harvey, J.S., Jr., & Sharkey, B.J. (1980). *Coaching young athletes.* Champaign, IL: Human Kinetics.

Medicine (1978, Fall). University of Washington School of Medicine, **5**(3), 6.

Miller v. Cloidt and Board of Education of the Borough of Chatham, No. L7241-62 (N.J. Super. Ct. 1964). Quoted in Appenzeller, H. (1978), *Physical education and the law.* Charlottsville, VA: The Michie Co.

Mogabgab v. Orleans Parish School Board, La. App. 239 S. 2d 456 (1970).

Moody v. Cronin, 484 F. Supp. 270 (1979).

Morris, T.P. (1980). Sports and the law. *Oklahoma City University Law Review*, **5**, 659-682.

Nabozny v. Barnhill, 31 Ill. App. 3d 212, 334 N.E. 2d 258 (1975).

Narol, M.S., & Dédopoulos, S. (1980, January). Defamation: A guide to referees' rights. *Trial*, **16**, 42-44.

Narol, M.S., & Dedopoulos, S. (1980, March). Defamation: A guide to referees' rights. *Trial*, **16**, 18-21.

Narol, M.S., & Dedopoulos, S. (1979, March). Kill the umpire: A guide to referees' rights. *Trial*, **15**, 32-34.

Narol, M.S., & Dedopoulos, S. (1972, September 6). The officials' potential liability for injuries in sporting events. *The National Law Journal*, p. 20.

Nygaard, G., & Boone, T. (1981). *Law for physical educators and coaches*. Salt Lake City: Brighton Publishing Company.

Ostro, H. (1980, May-June). Legal liability and the athletic director. *Scholastic Coach*, **49**, 8.

Participants liability for injury to a fellow participant in an organized athletic event (1976). *Chicago-Kent Law Review*, **53**, 97-108.

Passantino v. Board of Education of the City of New York, 395 N.Y.S. 2d 628 (N.Y. App. Div. 1976).

Peterson, T.L., & Smith, S.A. (1980, Summer). The role of the lawyer on the playing field: Sports injury litigation. *Barrister*, **7**, 10.

Prosser, W.L. (1971). *Handbook of the law of torts* (4th ed.). St. Paul, MN: West Publishing Co.

Section 41-1-405 Montana Codes Annotated.

Sports and the law (1978, June). *Trial*, **14**, 24-32.

Sports litigation (1977, January). *Trial*, **13**, 21-29.

Stevens v. Central School District No. 1 of the town of Ramapo, 270 N.Y.S. 2d 23, App'd 21 N.Y. 2d 780, 288 N.Y.S. 2d 475, 235 N.E. 2d 448 (1966).

Styer v. Reading, 360 Pa. 212, 61 A. 2d 382 (1948).

Summers v. Milwaukie Union High School District No. 5, Or App. 481 P. 2d 369 (1971).

Title IX of the Educational Amendments Act of 1972. 20 U.S.C.S. Par. 1681 et. seq.—P.L. 92-318.

Tort liability for players in contact sports (1976, Fall). *University of Missouri-Kansas City Law Review*, **45**, 119-129.

True story of what happens when the big kids say "It's my football, and you'll either play by my rules or you won't play at all" (1976). *Nebraska Law Review*, **55**, 335-361.

Underwood, J. (1979). *The death of an American game*. Boston: Little Brown.

Van der Smissen, B. (1968). *Legal liability of cities and schools for injuries in recreation and parks*. Cincinnati: The W.H. Anderson Company. (Separate 1975 Supplement.)

Vendrell v. School District No. 26C Malheur County, 226 Or. 263, 360 P. 2d 282 (1961).

Weistart, J.C., & Lowell, C.H. (1979). *The law of sports*. Indianapolis: Bobbs-Merril Company.

Welch v. Dunsmuir Joint Union High School District, 326 P. 2d 633 (Cal. App. 1958).

Woodring v. Board of Education of Manhasset et al., App. Div. 435 N.Y.S. 2d 52 (1981).

Woolf, R.G. (1980, January 7). Courts coming down hard on excessively violent players. *The National Law Journal*, p. 20.

Wright v. San Bernardino High School District, 121 Cal. App. 342, 263 P. 2d 25 (1953).

Index